Leading While Being Led

Lessons from a Senior Enlisted Advisor

by

Sean Sweeney

Table of Contents

Foreword

By: Leo Jenkins

The only thing worth writing is the truth. So here's the truth. My name is Leo Jenkins. I knew Sean Sweeney before he was a leader. Together we were followers. We served together at the 3rd Ranger Battalion. I was his medic. We deployed together twice. My second deployment was his first. Sweeney was a good follower. When I left the military and he continued I would have said that he had leadership potential. Look at me, I was right.

For the sake of being honest, I do not have the pedigree of a great leader. I'm not a fan of all that pesky responsibility. Hell, I'm not even a very good follower. This is partially because I have extremely high standards for the type of person I will allow myself to be led by. That benchmark was set impossibly high by a man who both Sean Sweeney and I worked for at 3rd Ranger Battalion.

He was an exceptional leader, but it wasn't entirely obvious why. Generally speaking, he looked out for his guys. He was firm but fair. But there was more to it than that. And the "more to it," was something that I never really tried to put words to. However, I (and I believe the rest of the guys under this leader) would have followed him straight into hell's furnace. But why?

As I read this book I realized that all of the attributes that Sweeney writes about fit that particular leader. He was exceptional in the most arduous environments imaginable and under truly deadly circumstances. As I continued to read this book I found myself thinking of other people who have been in a position of authority over me, people I won't give the title of leader to. What became humorously obvious as I read is that none of those people embodied any of the qualities or characteristics listed herein.

What strikes me as particularly odd is that just about everything in this book seems like common sense AFTER you read it. It's not complicated. But, it's also not exactly obvious. And it certainly isn't innate behavior in most people. I'm sure Sweeney had to learn most of these things through trial and error as did our exceptional former leader. What's great is that Sean Sweeney has distilled these things into such a palatable and digestible book.

As I read, I couldn't help but think how valuable this book would be, not just for someone in a leadership position, but someone in a subordinate position. Mainly a person who will soon commission or enlist into the military. I say this for two reasons.

First, you will, regardless of how long you've been in the military, be placed into a leadership role. I was made squad leader in my first week of basic training. I wasn't looking for that responsibility, hell I didn't want the responsibility. But there it was, heavy in my hands and I had to figure out how to wield it as I stumbled along. I wish I had read this book before shipping off to basic training. It would have saved me more than one heartache.

Second, expectations. Expectations are a lot easier to meet (or exceed) when you know what they are. When you know the model your leader is using, it makes it infinitely easier to be an efficient and useful follower. The efficient and useful follower doesn't stay a follower for long. They tend to get promoted ahead of their peers.

I don't believe that the value of the lessons herein are exclusive to the military either. If you just landed your first job working at McDonalds, there's value in these pages. Even if you only read and embody the first two sections, you will certainly be promoted ahead of your peers.

Why do I care though? I don't work for anyone and no one works for me. I'm a creative, a writer, a poet. Once or twice a year I send a manuscript to my publisher. They print it or they don't. I work with me, for me. But, I am also a husband and a father.

The deeper I read, the more I realized that the hard earned and clearly delivered advice within this book is not just for the application of one's profession, but any leadership role you might find yourself in. It is my opinion that the most important of all leadership roles is that of a parent. Now, I'm biased because it's the only leadership role I occupy, but a single shitty parent can have a truly devastating impact on the world. (We've all sat in front of that obnoxious brat who won't shut up in the movie theater, keeps kicking the back of our chair with those sticky little feet. Thank poor leadership for that nightmare. Also, those new reclining seats are bad ass. Super cozy.) The point is, being a good parent is being a good leader. Being a good domestic partner is knowing when to be a good leader and knowing when to be a good follower. Every person in a long term relationship is a led leader.

Alright, alright. I'm fixing to wrap this up so you can get to the knowledge nuggets that Sweeney scattered all across these pages. I know that's what you came for. I will end by saying, if you are a leader, a follower, a parent, or a person trying to be a slightly better version of yesteryou, (I made that up, it's not a real word.) just keep turning the pages. You have no excuse. The book is literally already in your hand.

Introduction

This book intends to provide you with ideas for improving your organization, whether military or civilian. The concepts I have learned and am attempting to articulate have taken nearly 20 years. They apply to nearly any level of leadership with minor modifications and should provide a framework for those thrust into a position for which they were unprepared. This collection of teachings is not intended to reinvent the wheel; rather, it is intended to get the gears in your head turning in order to come up with solutions that did not appear obvious at first.

This isn't a get-rich-quick guide. Nothing in this selection of teachings can be understood or applied unless they are constantly implemented and tested. It is not intended to be a guide for individual success but rather to assist teams in becoming more cohesive, successful, and competent in their daily work. Some of the suggestions in this section can be implemented quickly, but don't be misled: this is not a quick fix for your inherent flaws.

I have served about two decades in the Army and have held numerous leadership positions throughout my career. I've had the honor of serving with units as prestigious as the 75th Ranger Regiment (3/75), as storied as the 1st Infantry Division and the 173rd Airborne Brigade

(2/503), and as stoic as the 3rd Infantry Regiment (The Old Guard). I've also been assigned as a Drill Sergeant, training the next generation of warriors, and as an Army ROTC Instructor, teaching and mentoring the next generation of officers charged with leading America's sons and daughters against its enemies.

I've both led Soldiers into battle and been led into battle. I've jumped out of perfectly good planes carrying over 100 pounds of gear in the middle of the night and walked up and down 10,000-foot mountains on little to no sleep. I've conducted raids nearly every night of a 90-day rotational deployment and been away from family for more than a year at a time on other deployments. I've held numerous positions in each of these examples and within each of these units where people's lives depended on me, and mine depended on them. The lessons I've learned and that others have taught me have led me to success in these positions.

I am not a motivational speaker, nor am I the most knowledgeable person in the room. I am not a writer, and it took me over two years to complete this book. I have trouble focusing for long periods of time, so it was completed in spurts. As a result, there will be errors, poor word choices, and grammatical errors, despite my best efforts to minimize them. Some of the items in this book might even come off as cringy, outdated, or arrogant. I'm not a writer, once again.

I lack the clout of celebrity influencers like David Goggins and Jocko Willink. I've never been to Bud/s or served in a special operations unit for more than two years, and as such, I lack the projection ability that they have to help assist you in breaking down your self-imposed limits. That does not characterize me.

I'm not a leadership mentor or motivational speaker like Simon Sinek or Tony Robbins. I won't be able to persuade you to expect more from yourself. I am not Dave Ramsey, though I appreciate what he teaches to some extent. I cannot assist you in quickly getting out of debt and saving for retirement. I'd simply refer you to Dave and his team. I don't know as much about marketing and branding like Gary Vaynerchuk, so that's out as well. I am not a war hero in the same way that Alvin C. York, Audie Murphy, or Michael Murphy are. I am not a General in command of thousands of men and women, nor have I ever desired to be one. There is no way I could have been or ever will be a professional athlete, actor, or acclaimed singer (although I can belt out the *Bubble Guppies* and *Bluey* theme songs like a boss and 'Separate Ways' by Journey when necessary).

All the people mentioned above have excellent advice for everyone and have inspired millions of people to improve their daily lives and current situations. I've learned something from each of them, as well as from many other influential people in my life who have helped shape me into the person I am today.

So, why should you read this book if I am not any of those things? Why should you be interested in what I have to say?

Even though I have not been "the best" at anything, and very few people are, I have been very successful in each position to which I have been assigned. Granted, I don't have the street cred of a 20-year US Navy Seal when it comes to finding motivation when all hope seems lost. I'm not the "Rogue Warrior" Richard Marcinko or the Ultramarathon Man Dean Karnazes, but I'd like to think I've helped others learn to expect more from themselves and their teams.

There is a significant difference between completing a task with a team of like-minded individuals (Delta / Navy Seals / Air Force PJs, for example) and completing a task with a team from diverse backgrounds, abilities, and mindsets. For the most part, it wasn't an option for me to remove people from my organization when they failed to meet the stated standards. If someone was not up to the task at hand, I had to assist them in reaching the competency level required for their position. I didn't have the luxury of employing hand-picked, highly qualified Alpha-male meat-eaters. Even though I've had the privilege of working with some extremely motivated individuals who could hold their own in any position they desired, this was not always the case.

I've successfully brought together a diverse group of people with varying levels of competency, intelligence, fitness, confidence, and experience to achieve a goal. This is not to say that those in other special operations units or with different missions would not have been successful in the same way that I was, but their mission sets were far more focused and precise. I believe I have done a better job than most at motivating the unmotivated, teaching the unteachable, and getting stubborn personalities to change their mindsets and be open to new ideas.

The ability to put oneself to the test on a regular basis in various areas and positions appears to be the key to success and is critical to becoming more well-rounded. There's something special about being able to transition to any position successfully. It's amazing to be able to apply a principle learned in one location to the scope of another once you realize the connection.

So, with that said, I would encourage you to put what I've learned over the last two decades to the test for yourself and your organization. Use it to help your junior leaders understand what is expected of them. It can be used as a quick reference to discover new ways to reach the unreachable.

I want you to improve. I want your company to improve. I want you to be a better person tomorrow than you are today. I want you to work hard to become a better leader, husband, wife, father, mother, and boss. Allow my struggles, failures, and successes to teach you so you don't have to figure them out on your own. There's no need to reinvent the wheel or learn how to tie your shoes all over again. You are welcome to use my wheel, and I will tie your shoes for you.

I hope this helps you on your path to greatness or, at the very least, provides guidance when none has been provided.

LFG!

Chapter 1
DO. YOUR. DAMN. JOB.

"You've just got to go out there and do your job. You can't let other things get into your mind. We've all got jobs, and we've got to focus on our jobs." – Jermaine Wiggins

What does "do your damn job" mean? It means exactly what it says. Where's the confusion? I don't see it. If something falls within your scope or near your scope, it should be a no-brainer for you actually to do that thing. If it falls within your responsibilities, stop being lazy and DO IT!

I was just a lowly Private in the 3rd Ranger Battalion fresh off my second deployment, this time to Iraq. We were just getting ready to start conducting fixed-wing operations, which included conducting airfield seizure training. I had done this before and knew what to do during the training. We had just received several brand-new Rangers fresh out of the Ranger Indoctrination Program, and they had no clue what was going on.

Another lower enlisted Ranger and I took it upon ourselves to start teaching these young Rangers how we would conduct the upcoming training. No one had told us to do it. No one had threatened us with punishment (although that was always on the table). No one coerced or persuaded us to train these baby Rangers. We just did it because it was our damn job. We needed them to understand what to do just as much as we did, and we took pride in bringing them aboard.

Our lives are full of daily interactions with people who don't understand that they can be successful if they choose to do one simple thing…THEIR DAMN JOB! This is a very simple concept that, for some reason, not many people actually grasp. Doing your job can be as simple as being on time to work, submitting paperwork on time, or even going out of your way to get simple tasks done that make everyone else's job easier. As a leader, fuck that…as a manager, fuck that too…as a *person* who lives on this planet, you have a job to do. It is in your best interests to do it and do it well.

Doing your job is simple. Here's an example.

Let's say you are late for work because of traffic that was caused by an accident. I think that's something most of us have or will have to experience. If the driver/s of the vehicle/s in the accident had done their job, there would not have been an accident. How does a driver do their job, you ask? Simple. They obey the traffic laws, wear their seatbelts, have proper insurance and car registration, ensure they have done proper maintenance and have fuel, are aware of their surroundings, understand what blind spots are, use their turn signals, etc.

Now, a traffic light malfunctioning could have caused this accident. How does this play into the situation, you ask? Simple. The person installing the light might have forgotten to install some sort of weatherproof barrier for the wiring, or the hole might not have been dug deep enough for the pole. The person installing the circuit or controlling the timing of the light might have installed the wrong one or did not adjust it appropriately. Maybe the person making the circuit board or the person running the automated machine making it, or maybe even that guy's boss, did not properly inspect them before shipping them out to the installer.

This horrible example shows how people not doing their jobs can affect an entire situation in the here and now. Most jobs have a duty and scope assigned to them, which should at least guide you to what right looks like. Stop ignoring faults and fix them.

So, you don't get paid enough...that sucks, DYDJ.

So, you don't like your job...that sucks! Quit or DYDJ.

You keep getting chewed out by your boss for submitting bad products...boo hoo, DYDJ.

Your kids keep getting in trouble at school...you're a parent, so DYDJ and discipline them.

You're not getting the recognition you think you deserve at work, at home, or on the playing field...who gives a shit? DYDJ.

You've done everything that's been asked of you, and things are not seeming to work out for you…suck it up, it happens…DYDJ.

You are overworked and don't see a problem with cutting corners occasionally to speed up productivity…stop being lazy and DYDJ.

You're on security for a raid but are exhausted…suck it up, and DYDJ, people's lives depend on it.

Your subordinates are not completing tasks on time…look inward, evaluate the situation, and DYDJ.

Stop ignoring simple fixes in your life. This includes both your personal and professional lives. Stop walking by the shopping cart that's not in the stall and push it back. Stop accepting mediocrity from yourself and your subordinates because of "that's how we have always done it" talk. Stop letting lazy people infect you with their mediocrity. Who gives a shit if you're placed in the right fielder equivalent in your place of work? You're THE right fielder, so DYDJ, and do it well.

Here are some other helpful hints if you still don't understand what it means to do your damn job:

Process that paperwork that you were supposed to process yesterday.

Fix the recurring mistakes you've seen in those emails, letters, paperwork, etc.

Get up and run…stop hitting the snooze button.

Play with your kids.

Discipline your kids.

Complete your work on time.

Everything in this world would run more efficiently and be more functional if everyone did their damn job.

If you tell someone that you will get back to them about something…GET BACK TO THEM.

If you tell someone that you will call them back…CALL THEM BACK.

Nothing about doing one's job is hard except the inherent laziness of being a human. If you forgot something, that's because you didn't write it down.

We ignore countless things in our daily lives that can help others be more productive. All the things that you have been pushing until tomorrow or hoping no one will notice, fix it today. All that paperwork you have been taking your time completing because it takes too much time, finish it! You need to be better because others can't be better without you.

Take pride in who you are as a person who lives on this planet. Even if you hate your job, do it! Do it with pride. Stop being a lazy sack of crap and do your damn job.

Chapter 2

The Four Rights

"Integrity is doing the right thing, even when no one is watching." – C.S. Lewis

The Four Rights are a simple internal check one can use to ensure they are staying on task. While simple at their core, they do require you to perform. They are as follows: be at the RIGHT place, at the RIGHT time, in the RIGHT uniform, and doing the RIGHT thing.

Being in the right place means being at the exact location you need to be at. This sounds like a simple concept, but people often don't know where they are supposed to be at any given time. To fix this, one should always remember to plan ahead and know where you must be before you must be there. Being at the right place might require conducting a reconnaissance before your arrival. Reconnaissance can be as simple as looking at a map to get your bearings or as elaborate as going to the actual site beforehand. Within this, being at the right place also includes being at the right place within the right place, meaning the correct room or office within the building.

In the military, being on time does not actually mean being on time. What it really means is to be several minutes early. This allows a buffer period should any unforeseen issues arise. Being early also shows respect for those you are about to address while simultaneously exhibiting time management and planning skills. So, always remember to be early.

First impressions are lasting impressions for many people. So, being in the right uniform is of vital importance. You would not go outside for a hike wearing a ball gown...or would you? This could mean anything from being in your full camouflage uniform to being in the correct physical fitness uniform. If you're attending a corporate function, being in business-casual might be okay for some occasions but not formal enough for others. You may have to ask others for the appropriate attire for a given situation. Don't assume you will always know. Your clothes say a lot about who you are as a person, and how you wear them shows how much you care, so take pride in your appearance and be in the appropriate uniform.

Doing the right thing sounds very simple at its base, but for some people, they might not know what the right thing is. For our purposes, the right thing does not mean what is morally, ethically, or legally right but what your job is at that given time. For instance, if you are on guard duty or something of the sort, your job is to guard. Do your job, go around, do your checks, make sure everybody is doing what they are supposed to be doing, and make sure that you are doing what you are supposed to be doing. If there are instructions that you must know, read the freaking instructions. If there is something you are supposed to check, turn in or do...do it. Doing the right thing is easy for most people, and it is very clear to them what the right thing to do is, but in our laziness and self-centeredness, we deliberately choose not to do it. Don't be that lazy POS.

Applying the 4 R's will allow you to accomplish your tasks in a set order without missing any major points. Enforcing this with your subordinates is a very simple procedure. Just go down that checklist and ask them when you believe they are off task; more times than not, they will fix themselves without being instructed. Simply ask them, "Where are you supposed to be right now?" or "What are you supposed to be wearing for this function?," or "What should you be doing right now?"

These simple questions can and will often spur some discussion, so you can easily help them transition back to what their focus should be at that time.

Chapter 3

Lead From the Front

"A leader is someone who has a clear vision (knows the way), follows that vision, (goes the way) and helps others to find their path (shows the way)." – John C. Maxwell

"You lead from the front!" is a quote from Audie Leon Murphy that encapsulates what it means to be a leader. Not a boss, a leader. This comes in many different forms whether you're in the military, in an office-type setting, or just within your family in general. Murphy was one of the most highly decorated Soldiers in American history, earning every single medal for Valor that the United States of America has, up to and including the Medal of Honor. This famous quote should be at the forefront of every interaction or encounter a leader has with their subordinates.

Leading cannot be done from behind a desk. It cannot be done from behind the front lines. It cannot be done from your office without interaction with your subordinates. Leading requires you to be at the point of friction for your team. It requires you to see first-hand what is going on in the trenches. Context is lost via email, phone calls, and second-hand briefings. The best oral storytellers could not give a leader all the context for every situation. An artist cannot paint if they do not have paint or are in the dark.

This concept is simple at its face value. How hard can it be to place oneself at the front of any organizational issues? There are different approaches that must be followed whether you're in the military, a civilian, or when it comes to family.

Let's explore those ideas.

Leading from the front in the military

The military defines leadership as "the process of influencing people by providing purpose, direction, and motivation while operating to accomplish the mission and improve the organization." Providing purpose is, in effect, why said task needs to be done or why an objective needs to be met. This flattening of communication shows your subordinates your thought process as a leader and your priorities. Leaders in the military need to be on the ground with their men and women to gather all the information they require to make an informed decision. Being present as a leader is vital. Just showing your subordinates and peers that you are willing to do what you ask them and placing yourself in danger builds that confidence within the ranks. Their trust in you will increase, and their resolve will harden to reach your objectives.

Leading from the front in the civilian sector

Being a leader in the civilian sector can mean many different things. It could be that you are a supervisor for a construction company. Maybe it means you are the assistant manager of a fast-food restaurant. It could even mean you are the manager of a homeowner's association or leader of a church group. In all these instances, you must understand one key point: Be available for your subordinates. This availability builds trust and cohesion within your small subset of society. This is a way of leading from the front. Another way you can do this is by being at an important meeting instead of your deputy. Or maybe even going out to the worksite in the shitty weather to see how the environment affects your people. These little acts show that you care and can also provide you, as the leader, with clarity in your decision-making.

Leading from the front in your family

This involves having morals that your loved ones can always see emanating from you. Be strong in your conviction and be strong in your faith. Don't let that waiver; if it does, do whatever you can to get back on course. Show your kids that you are a force to be reckoned with and that your love is never-ending. Teach your family to give themselves to ethical causes. You show them this by doing it yourself. The world does not revolve around becoming rich and famous. It revolves around being stewards for our children and this world. You can't expect your kids to want to play a certain sport if you don't do it with them and make it fun. You can't expect your kids to do well in school if they never see you trying to better yourself. Don't ride on your laurels by saying, "When I was your age" or "I used to play this or that instrument or sport" or "I was a part of this group". Your family will follow your lead. If you choose the right things to be passionate about, they will too.

All walks of life require leaders to have the mental toughness, intelligence, and morals attached to all their decisions. You cannot expect others to do what you say if you do not do it yourself. If you want others to be better at fitness, YOU must take it seriously. If you want others to take their faith seriously, YOU must take yours seriously. If you want others to turn paperwork in on time, YOU must also turn it in on time. That's the essence of leading from the front.

Being a good example to all people by making analytical decisions while not compromising your integrity is the sign of a strong leader. Civilian and military leaders alike have this potential. For some, it is a learned trait. Others possess it naturally. But no matter what, each must continue to work on that trait to remain a mentally sharp and trusted leader.

Chapter 4

Be a Good Follower

"He who cannot be a good follower, cannot be a good leader." – Aristotle

It has taken me years to realize all the lessons others have taught me, without being aware of it. One of the more influential ones that has driven me to this day was learned in Iraq and was taught in less than five seconds.

We were just inserted into a large open field on the outskirts of a small village in Iraq. The 160th Special Operations Aviation Regiment flew us in their CH-47s, and my platoon, of which I was still one of the junior Soldiers, was tagged to conduct a nighttime raid on a suspected high-value target. We brought the necessary breaching equipment with us aboard the aircraft, which included tools and, strangely enough, ladders (which we made sure were padded to muffle the noise they would make).

I had the distinct pleasure of carrying one myself which turned out to be an interesting movement to the target house. Just imagine seeing one of the deadliest military units in history moving through an open field, in the dead of night, looking like characters from *Call of Duty*, and carrying a damn 12-ft ladder you could buy from Lowes or Home Depot. We truly were a sight to see.

As we completed our movement, we began the typical nighttime raid setup. This includes setting up your security, support, and assault teams. You do this to ensure that the entire objective is cordoned off from outside threats, that there are enough key weapons systems supporting the assault teams' movement, and that the assault teams know exactly where the target house is.

Once security and support were set it was the assault teams' job to raid the objective. My squad, in which I was just a rifleman at the time, was tasked with being Assault 1. This meant that we were the primary squad for the initial breach of the objective house.

The initial breach for this mission called for using the ladder that I was carrying and climbing over the exterior wall of the compound. We moved up to the objective and immediately set up our ladders. My squad leader was the first one over the ladder and moved so quickly that the team that was supposed to be following him never made it over in time. I immediately climbed that ladder and was right on his heels after jumping from the top of the wall. Now it was just him and me behind the wall, with the rest of the platoon outside the compound slowly making their way over the wall.

While my squad leader was preparing to breach the door, one of the inhabitants came out to see what was happening. Once the person noticed that the reckoning had arrived, she (yes, SHE, we realized it was a woman after her scream) attempted to run back into the house, possibly to warn the others inside or maybe as a response to the fear she had from seeing several fully armed Americans with night vision and short barreled M4s staring at her. Without thinking, I sprinted for her, grabbed her arm, and held her back as the squad finally caught up, moved into their assault position, and began the breach. I handed her off to our trail squad and returned to my squad to move into the target house to complete our mission.

Now, you may wonder, "How is this a significant story?" The point is much subtler than the other topics in this book thus far. It was not my job to question my squad leader or wonder why he was moving ahead of the rest of the assault team without support, but I noticed that he needed a buddy with him and did not hesitate to jump off that wall and cover his movement. We never move alone, and if something happened to him while he was assessing his entry point, that would have been on all of us.

You must be a good follower before you can be a good leader, and even when you are the leader, you must trust that those beneath you will be there when the shit hits the fan. Now, this story shows that following others is one of the best ways to learn and become a better leader yourself. Let the leader lead. If asked, provide your unbiased opinion. If not asked, but warranted, provide your input or two cents. But the overall idea is to be good at following others. When others see you following without hesitation, they themselves will feel obligated to do the same. Your peers will take notice, and your seniors will also acknowledge it. Being a good follower shows those beneath you what is expected of them and desired within your organization. Good followers can and do turn into great leaders. Sometimes blind following is necessary as a follower, but your pride cannot precede the mission or task at hand.

Chapter 5

Perception vs. Intention

"The reality of life is that your perceptions – right or wrong – influence everything else you do. When you get a proper perspective of your perceptions, you may be surprised how many other things fall into place." – Roger Birkman

This is a hot topic in every aspect of our lives today, or at least the media thinks it is. Either way, having a well-rounded opinion on this topic is important. It should help clear the fog of war that clouds our minds when something is said or done that affects others differently than how we expected.

As a leader in any facet (this means top, middle, and low-level leaders), we must ensure those who hear us speak to understand what we are saying. Not just philosophically but also contextually. They need to know why we said a specific thing and what we meant by that thing. What could have been a well-intentioned statement might have been perceived as being cold, heartless, or biased.

When making statements that can be perceived differently by people with different beliefs or thought processes, it is important to have that statement reviewed by others who share those beliefs. This ensures that as many issues as possible are found and can be addressed if need be saving time on the back end.

For example, during the BLM/George Floyd protests/riots (whichever word you choose to use), our unit was given the task of potentially assisting local law enforcement...NON-lethally. However, this caused some issues within the formation as a significant portion of the unit agreed with the stated issues that the movement was trying to bring to light. With this taken into account and reflecting on it now, it would have been a good idea had the command brought some of those who had that though process into the planning process so that the Commander's overall intent was communicated and understood without people questioning their motives.

While a leader cannot realistically control the emotions of their audience with respect to the leader's actions or words, that leader can control how they project that information.

On the other hand, leaders and subordinates need to understand that how they feel initially might not be the correct response, as what they perceive as an injustice, an attack on them, or a skewed statement, might just be a lack of internal understanding. What the speaker said might have been wrongly contextualized by the receiver. It is important not to rush to judgment until all the variables are discussed, the fog has settled, and clarifications have been made.

Regardless of who was right or wrong, everyone (leader and subordinates) needs to ensure that their intentions are known and that how they perceive it is known to the speaker. This is true in all forms of communication, including email, phones, texts, and messengers. The intention of the communication needs to be clearly stated, and the perception of the communication needs to be understood after the communication has been made.

This is not to argue that one side is more important than the other; however, in my experience as a leader, I had to be willing to hear arguments on how my interactions were perceived by people of all different backgrounds and assignments. I also had to consider how my actions were perceived outside of my organization and by my boss's boss. This would theoretically be the case in most other organizations. If my intentions were not clearly visible, I would have no reason to be angered by a wrongly perceived perspective.

Be willing to explain your intentions when you email, call, text, or send a messenger to provide information. If you are the receiver, ensure you understand the intention and don't rush to judgment because it's probably incorrect.

Chapter 6

Systems Processes and People Processes

"If you can't describe what you are doing as a process, you don't know what you're doing." – W. Edwards Deming

Systems are important in ensuring there is continuity and that we are not learning from scratch every time someone departs. People processes are also important as they can be seen as an untapped resource. Their personal system might be more effective than your system. Everyone has different ideas, and everyone sees things in a different spectrum. Use this to your advantage.

We have so much turnover in our military that we cannot operate without systems in place to manage it. These systems stand the test of time and are there long before you arrive and long after you leave. They are always evolving but strangely stay the same in the sense that they are always trying to provide the Commander with enough information to make a decision.

People processes are what individuals use to make their specific job easier, more productive, and more fluid. They are specific to each individual, and since everyone is wired differently, their process will differ from the next individual. What I see as vital, another might see as erroneous. These can include using formulas in Microsoft Excel, using a specific format for paperwork, or a specific data tracking metric. The individual metrics are as varied and unique as the person implementing them.

But what happens if that person leaves or cannot do their job? What happens if they get promoted? What happens if they get reassigned? What happens if they cease to exist...you know...DIE? That is the reason why system processes need to be emplaced to ensure there is continuity within your organization for the foreseeable future and to help withstand the numerous storms that affect units, organizations, and businesses all the time.

I used my own personal tracking system depending on what position I was filling at that time and depending on what the objective or plan was. It's not set in stone that I had to stick to a specific protocol. God knows the military has these for days, but I do use tracking mechanisms and paperwork that those before have used to make my job easier. I have also let others use their own internal processes, but I did have them make a handover book to give to the next person who eventually replaced them. It would include names of personnel and their job, locations of key places or offices, what the daily, weekly, monthly, and yearly schedule looked like, and what were our big events that we typically did. This kept me on schedule and helped create a framework that I could use to brief the next person taking over for me.

I am an advocate of people using their personal system to make their job easier. As a leader, you must ensure those using those systems have the framework for their process written down or within a handover or continuity book to ensure the person now filling that role can quickly get up to speed. This is not a nice to have thing in your organization, it is a NEED-to-have thing in your organization. Don't wait until the unthinkable happens before you have a plan in place. BE proactive.

Chapter 7

Consistency

"In baseball, my theory is to strive for consistency, not to worry about the numbers. If you dwell on statistics, you get shortsighted, if you aim for consistency, the numbers will be there at the end."
– Tom Seaver

You will not get that beach body overnight or by working out for one week. You will not become the CEO of a billion-dollar company without knowing your business and market. You will not be a professional soccer player by only practicing when you feel like it. Nothing noteworthy is going to happen to you or for you if you are not invested in your goal and don't constantly practice ways to achieve it. Being consistent in our daily lives shows a level of self-control, a level of maturity, and a level of intrinsic motivation that sadly, many people do not have.

As a Soldier, I have had to take countless fitness assessments throughout my career, including running, pushups, pullups, sit-ups, and a variety of other activities. If I only started training for these assessments the week prior to them, I would not have been ready for them when the time came. It takes months and years of physical training to get to the point where I could make a decent showing at these events. It didn't happen overnight. Sure, some people have a natural gift for these things but for me, I had to work at. You should expect that too.

In addition to having to be in shape for the physical demands of my job, I had to have a broad knowledge of everything that applied to my specialty, from shooting and communications, to interpersonal tact and resilience. None of those are easy to learn over just a short amount of time. It took a constant influx of information and training to get it to stick and still requires maintenance to this day to remain useful.

Short bursts of energy are great if the mission calls for that immediate dynamism, but slow and steady wins the race. People should know what to expect of you for the most part. Your consistency in your daily actions shows your reliability to outside suitors. They will know that they can trust that you will be a constant sponge for information and that you will continue to better yourself throughout the years.

There is also something to be said about being consistent with your interactions with people, especially those who are subordinate to you. You must treat all of them the same. This is not saying you must treat them with padded gloves all the time but your thought processes in how you deal with each of them should be the same.

Everyone has different things they are good at, and a good leader takes advantage of this. What I am advocating for is that when a subordinate has a similar issue that another had, you should apply the same mindset and decision-making process to that problem. If the result turns out to be different, so be it. You do not owe an explanation for applying your standards if they are consistent.

Chapter 8

No One Knows Everything

"It's possible to both know and not know something." – Emily St. John Mandel

Don't fall into the downward spiral of thinking that one particular person knows everything. It will undoubtedly lead you to only seeing one perspective on things and not actually performing some critical thinking, especially with your internal decision-making process.

You will encounter many people who believe they are God's gift to humanity or someone who consistently rests on their laurels because no one dares question them. You may even run into someone who has been successful at everything they have done in their career, so you start to think, "Why not just do it their way?" While this seems effective since they have had a strong run thus far, it is flawed thinking.

The world is full of well-read people who have PhDs, people who are experts within a specific field of study, professional athletes, award-winning musicians, and writers. Not a single one of them knows everything.

Within the military you will run into people who have these same characteristics. They have been to this training, or have served in these units, or been deployed to this location, or they attended this school or that school. Anywhere you go you must understand that no matter how much training someone has had, the best ideas may not always come from them.

Don't be hesitant to share your idea or technique, even with those who are supposed experts. Even if they choose not to use your idea then, you could influence others to speak up by making yourself the catalyst for them to follow suit. By speaking up, you also let others know that you are in it to win it and are not scared to voice your concerns, which is a valuable quality to have in both corporate and leadership settings.

In my career, I was rarely the most well-versed person on certain topics. There was always someone who knew more than me. This taught me to remain open-minded and more willing to accept other ideas, even if I was fairly certain there were better options.

Leaders in the military rely on the expertise of those they lead to accomplish the mission. I was able to do this by leveraging the strengths of those within the unit. When I was serving as a First Sergeant in the Old Guard, we had a very specialized ceremonial mission to conduct daily. To accomplish this, we had a team of ceremonial leaders that were experts in their field. They knew the protocol for all military related events from basic marching up to and including a Presidential Inauguration. These hand-selected people were the best the Army had to offer and did their job with the utmost professionalism.

Even though I outranked them in principle and pay grade, these people were the only ones who could certify or decertify anyone within the unit on ceremonial tasks, and holy crap there were a lot of them. This included decertifying the unit Commander if they did not do their job right...which did happen. As a leader, I had to swallow my pride and recognize that I was not THE GUY for that specific job. Someone else was better suited than me for it even though I had been fairly successful in my career up until that point.

This is the case for many of the most successful people who have lived. Presidents choose their cabinet based on a wide variety of skills that they deem necessary to accomplish a specific task within their agenda. These people usually have some experience in the field and are experts at something related to the job that is being asked of them. For example, it makes zero sense to have a first-generation farmer from Utah act as the Secretary of Defense, but it might make sense if that farmer was a 3rd or 4th generation farmer with a degree in agriculture to be the secretary of agriculture.

We could use countless examples, but the point is a great basketball player does not make a great truck driver. A great businessman does not make a great truck driver. A person with a Harvard degree does not make a great businessman. All of these are learned, and it's best to choose your team based upon the strengths of individuals. Know your team and come to the realization that you are not the expert at everything, even if you do have all the credentials that say so. Be humble about what you know and be curious about what others know. There's almost certainly a better solution out there for your problem.

Chapter 9

The Golden Rule is Bullshit…Sort of

"Don't treat people badly, treat them accordingly."
– Unknown

Treat everyone the way you wish to be treated. That sounds right, or at least fair, doesn't it? It works awesome for kids and establishes a foundation of understanding that can be built upon later. However, In my experience, this is not the be all or end all. Sure, it's a good start, but there is a point where someone may not want to be treated how you want to be treated. Depending on the circumstances, they may want to be treated easier or harsher. Hell, even their upbringing and experiences may influence how they believe they should be treated.

Everyone deserves to be treated in accordance with their actions, not according to how you feel you should be treated if the roles were reversed. An individual's actions should be the defining indicator.

Here's a quick example.

I had the pleasure of being a Drill Sergeant for three "glorious" years. The lessons I learned there have shaped how I interact with everyone: family, friends, acquaintances, and strangers. We were charged with training the next generation of recruits in all the basic skill level one tasks that all Soldiers must know, including shooting their weapons, maneuvering on the battlefield, performing first aid, and being able to receive and execute orders quickly. Needless to say, it was much more fun for us Drill Sergeants than for our recruits.

Upon receiving a new cycle of recruits, the first task is to establish yourself as the subject matter expert and break all their perceived limits from physical to mental and everything in between. We dealt with people from all walks of life, the inner city, good ole boys from the south, daddy's girls, only children, one of eight, family tradition, etc. All these young Americans raised their right hand and took an oath to defend the constitution of the United States against all enemies. Our job was to mold them into well-trained Soldiers capable of meeting any enemy that our country deemed a threat.

To establish ourselves as the big dogs, we immediately conducted what is known as a shark attack. Basically, it involves all the Drill Sergeants yelling commands simultaneously to confuse, frighten, and upset the recruits' senses. This was done so that we could break everything they thought they knew about themselves. We needed to be able to start from scratch with them. It was a necessary evil that was wildly effective at giving us our desired result in due time.

How does this example support the golden rule being BS, you ask?

Here's a quick story to explain it.

When I went through basic training, I expected the Drill Sergeants to be mean SOBs, and barring some rare instances, they were. I wanted them to stop yelling at me and let me rest when my body was tired. I wanted them to care when I didn't feel good and let me call home whenever I wanted. NONE of that happened, and it seems that those tactics worked. If they had stopped when we got tired, were hungry, or didn't feel good, we would have never been able to reach graduation, much less become an effective Infantryman.

The golden rule says that you should treat others how you wish to be treated. In those moments, no one wants to be treated the way we treated the recruits. As a Drill Sergeant, you treat everyone the same and how they should be treated, not how you want to be treated. We treated them accordingly, much like an extremely strict parent, but it all supported a goal. Making them into Soldiers.

This does not mean you should treat people like crap unless they show you they are worthy of being treated better. It means that their actions should be the defining characteristic of how you treat them. This does not mean you are a bad person. In fact, it can teach others that their actions have consequences that they may not have intended.

The whole Golden Rule idea is great for little kids, as mentioned earlier, but for everyone else, treat them how they should be treated in accordance with their actions.

Chapter 10

You Can't Be Anything You Want to Be

"You cannot be anything you want to be – but you can be a whole lot more of who you already are." – Tom Rath

I am a 5-foot 9-inch physical specimen of a man. I have a Greek god's body and the mind of a brilliant scientist. Even knowing this, there is no way I would be the starting center for the Philadelphia 76ers or the starting defensive end for the Chicago Bears. It is just not genetically in the cards for me.

This is an example of my physical body and upbringing not being in line with my fake aspirations of becoming a professional sports player. Yes, I know, there are several positions in which my stature would fit right in. I could, for example, be a defensive back in the NFL, a major league baseball player, a hockey player, a basketball guard, or even an Olympic gymnast. What I cannot be is a position that is historically not suited to my size. In baseball, that would be first base. In hockey, that may be a center or defenseman. In basketball, that would be center or forward. And in football, that would be a lineman or linebacker.

This also applies to other professions as well such as lawyer, doctor, or astronaut. For instance, it makes no sense for me to try becoming an astronaut without having a STEM degree or hundreds/thousands of hours as a jet pilot. I always try to understand my current mental and physical limitations. Granted, hard work and dedication might play a huge factor, but so does having the right intangibles, such as intellectual capacity, likeability, and interpersonal skills. Now, I could train like a madman to get myself into the perfect physical shape or even study hard and possibly earn a perfect 4.0 GPA in college, but that does not mean I truly understand the topics at hand. There are some topics that I am not destined to be very good at.

This is not to say that we should crush all our kids' hopes and dreams and tell them that they can't be astronauts, doctors, or pro sports players. In fact, it supports the opposite of that. Give your kids the motivation to try hard while they are young. As they mature, your approach should be adjusted as their intellectual capacity grows and their bodies adjust to an adult's. As this starts, you need to provide more and more ideas and examples for your children to make better decisions about what they'd like to do when they grow up without telling them their dreams are dumb.

In the military, I cannot become a Navy Seal or Delta Force Operator. Sure, maybe at one time I may have been in the physical and mental shape to do it, but now, not so much. Time has the innate ability to give perspective and temper your optimism. That can be a good thing. Come to terms with that fact sooner rather than later, and you will be a much happier person and leader. Everyone has a job to do in the grand scheme of things. That job doesn't have to be glamorous, but it needs to be done.

In the civilian world, not everyone can become a neurologist. As discussed earlier, YES, studying hard and taking all the right courses would help with this, but only so many positions are available for these highly specialized jobs. Being content with being a family practice doctor might be more suitable for most people.

This does not mean you are a failure but rather it might mean that you have met your potential as a human being. The whole "everyone has unlimited potential" argument is bullshit. Once you meet your potential, your life will get easier. The tough part is understanding when you meet it. Be happy with where you are. Still continue to study and train hard but come to terms with the idea of being physically, intellectually, or professionally at your limit. It's OK. Not everyone can or should be anything they want.

Chapter 11

Leadership Not Likership…Mostly

"I want people to be afraid of how much they love me." – Michael Scott (Steve Carell)

As a leader within the military community, you are responsible for everything that your unit does or fails to do. That means that if your Soldiers did an awesome job at the most recent training event, you did an awesome job at that event. But by the same token, if your Soldiers forgot to turn in paperwork on time, YOU forgot to turn paperwork in on time. There is no limit to this thinking so you must learn to embrace it and learn from it.

I have skirted this issue for my entire career as a Soldier. My upbringing has led me to find humor in nearly every situation. My time in the military has expanded this to include situations that to the normal person would seem inappropriate. Maybe it's a coping mechanism…Either way, it's a part of my leadership style now.

I have been chewed out by superiors for being too "nice" to my Soldiers and too buddy-buddy with them. I have also been admonished for being too hard on my Soldiers up to and including an investigation…unfounded of course. But this just shows that it can be a tough job in any setting, being a leader and all. You need to know what makes your Soldiers tick and how to motivate them to do the right thing and complete their missions without being told.

When first being placed in a position of influence over others, leaders have an obligation to do everything they can to get the most out of those in their charge if the means are legally, morally, and ethically sound. It also means that you will always face the awkward predicament of either being liked or being a leader as these two will often be opposed to each other.

A leader will have to make the hard choices for their subordinates and place mission accomplishment on a pedestal. Should that leader release their Soldiers early to reward them for a job well done or should they make them stay until all weapons and equipment are spotless and checked for functionality? The leader who is more concerned with being liked may err on the side of releasing the Soldiers while the leader concerned with being a leader may make their Soldiers stay until every box is checked.

What I would suggest is that there is no cookie cutter answer to this dilemma. Each situation requires one to consider all the contributing factors. A leader has the tough job of finding the middle ground to many dilemmas that they are posed with. They are the link between the subordinates and the higher command. They must both please their superiors and keep their organization motivated. It is not an easy job.

Likership in this sense revolves around the leader striving to be liked more than being a leader. It is a necessary evil that all leaders need to possess. Though many do not. Being a likable person seems simple, yet many people cannot figure it out. Empathy goes a long way in this situation. Humor plays a big part as well. I have dealt with leaders that cannot comprehend why humor is so important to an organization and, needless to say, they were not very well received. This can probably be attributed to the old school stoicism that they believe all military leaders should have.

Now, the fine line between the two is hard to see at times. A leader can be liked all day and not be an effective leader and a leader can be effective at their job while not being liked. Both are required of leaders in the military and civilian life. Sure, one can become successful without being liked and many people can be liked without being successful. But if a leader wants to be respected by their men, feared by their enemies, exude confidence, and have their finger on the pulse of the organization, they need to be liked on a personal level by their subordinates and peers. It's not an easy thing to work for someone who you wholeheartedly do not like...believe me, I have had many leaders such as this...hell, I could have been that leader to some poor soul.

When push comes to shove, your subordinates will go out of their way and go above and beyond for you when you are liked, so likership is an undervalued trait that a leader must have. If you are not of that persuasion, you will find that it takes a lot more effort on your part to get things done than the leader who is actually liked by their subordinates.

Chapter 12

Empathy vs. Sympathy

"Empathy is seeing with the eyes of another, listening with the ears of another and feeling with the heart of another." – Alfred Adler

Empathy is defined as the ability to understand and share the feelings of another person. Sympathy has several definitions but the one we will focus on is "the formal expression of pity or sorrow for someone else's misfortune." Whereas empathy is understanding another's feelings, sympathy means you are expressing that other person's feelings.

Why is knowing these two words and their difference important for a leader, you ask?

It's important because as a leader you need to know how your subordinates are feeling in regards to how they are acting. Being an empathetic leader shows that you care about their well-being without emanating those feelings. Being a sympathetic leader in this context means you are sharing in the pain that your subordinates are having.

These two do not mean the same thing. Leaders need to remain empathetic, not sympathetic for most of their job. Sympathy is more aligned with family and close friends. Empathy includes family, close friends, acquaintances, colleagues, and the like. Being able to understand why your employees or subordinates feel a certain way comes with experience. It can be both a learned trait as well as something one is born with. Either way, it does play a significant role in being a good leader.

If you have a subordinate who is about to be reprimanded for something they did wrong, you, as the leader, need to remain empathetic to their situation. Understand the feelings that could be going through their head and emotions that they are displaying. It is not your job to be sympathetic to them. That is the role of their inner circle. In order to remain unbiased and have a clear head for decision making, empathy is key. It allows your judgment to remain uncompromised by maintaining a slight separation from the person in question.

When leaders do not know the difference between these two terms, bad decisions are made based on emotion. Emotional decision making is usually a bad idea, especially in high stress environments. Understand how people are feeling. Understand how situations affect different people. But do not let sympathy cloud your judgment.

Chapter 13

Don't Be So Much of a Servant Leader That You Forget to Be a Leader

"Leadership is not about being in charge. Leadership is about taking care of those in your charge." – Simon Sinek

There is a theory in some organizations that being a good leader means you must be a servant to your subordinates. This is referred to as servant leadership. It does not mean that the subordinate Soldiers themselves oversee the unit or business but they do have a stake in how well it performs. Giving them what they need to accomplish their job is what is meant in this sense of being a servant leader. Where we inevitably run into issues is when all we do is give them what they need while ignoring what we need as leaders.

Everything falls on you as the leader if shit hits the fan. If you don't make the mission, YOU failed. If you miss a deadline, YOU failed. If someone is injured on your watch, YOU failed. That's the bane of being a leader. It is a glorious burden that all people in positions of power bear. The failures of those under their umbrella are the failure of the leader even if said leader was not able to influence the success of the mission at that time.

While the failures of the team are attributed to the person in charge, the success is also attributed to them. If anything deemed successful occurs on their watch, it looks great for them. It's a double-edged sword that they are wielding. It's not necessarily fair but that's just how it is. There's not much one can do to change this fact.

The servant leader approach is one that Robert Greenleaf pioneered in the 1970s. Many "new" leaders or those thrust into new positions tend to be at one extreme or the other when it comes to leadership. This can be attributed to a plethora of factors: Too many war movies growing up. Shitty upbringing. Listening to the wrong mentor...etc. The reasons can go on and on, but the result is the same, with them tending to fall into one of the extremes of being too hard or being too soft on their teams. It is only through trial and error that their leadership philosophy is molded and shaped more towards the middle ground.

Giving your subordinates what they need to complete their job is important to the success of the organization. If they don't have what they need, how can you expect them to get the work done? They are not you and you are not them. You are in that position for a reason. Act like it.

You can't simply give them the tools they need to be successful. You must also give them guidance and apply deliberate decision making to help them accomplish the mission. You must keep them on task. Keep them motivated. Keep them honest. Give them benchmarks. Give them deadlines. Punish in private. Praise in public. As a leader you must give them room to make mistakes but not wear kid gloves with them. Sometimes they need to hear the brutal truth and sometimes they need some empathy. Your job as a leader is to know when to adjust your approach to get your desired result – a result that should end in being more effective and efficient.

When I was in any position of influence or leadership position, I would receive the task to be done, assignment, or mission from my boss. At that point I would conduct some internal planning on my part to wrap my head around what was being asked of me. I would then pass the information down to my subordinates. This would be the Leader portion of my style. Next, I would ask what they needed from me to accomplish that task. This part was ongoing as things would come up periodically that they needed help or guidance with. This would be the servant part of my style. Finally, I would hold them accountable with what they had been tasked with by giving expectations and deadlines. This would get us back to the leader part of my philosophy. It worked great for me nearly every time I used it.

Apply a Lead-Serve-Lead principle in your philosophy and when accomplishing tasks. Each individual task can have its own application of this philosophy and the entire organization can apply it holistically as part of their daily interactions. There will be times when it is necessary to stray towards the extremes of either being "soft" or "hard," but realistically it's best to stay as close to the middle as possible. It's your job as the leader to figure out which one fits your current situation.

Chapter 14

Ignore Them and Their Opinions

"Care about people's approval, and you will always be their prisoner." – Lao Tzu

I have run into a lot of people throughout my military service that have made my career difficult, and left me questioning whether to continue the journey toward retirement. I have had people tell me I'm an idiot, wrong, childish, weak, immature, overrated, lazy, insecure etc. From their perspective, all these descriptions probably rang true. Who knows, maybe at that specific time, I was being those things, but one thing is certain, their opinions do not mean shit. Ignore them.

As a leader you are inevitably going to have people who you come across that are conniving, vindictive, self-serving, arrogant, liars, and overall, just bad human beings. There is not a damn thing you can do about it except just forget about them. If you have done what you need to do as the person in charge, if there is nothing more you can accomplish that day, then who gives a shit if someone says you're being lazy? Ignore them, their opinion does not mean shit.

There are times when you need to get to the grind and keep chugging along with life and there are times when it's ok to just chill. For the most part, you will fall somewhere in the middle of this since neither is sustainable.

When you overhear someone say you can't do something, ignore that negative crap and do it anyway.

When you are told that you're being too crazy, then if what you are doing is safe – ignore them, do it anyway.

If someone recommends something to you but you never asked them for it, ignore them and do what you were going to do anyway...unless they have a good idea, that is.

There is nothing you can do to change what has already been said or done with regards to you but you can control how you respond to others. That response is almost always a violence of action approach since their opinions do not mean shit. Stop caring what others think about you, your decisions, your family, your job, and your life. They don't own you. You're not their slave so, fuck them and their opinions.

The whole "sticks and stones may break my bones but words will never hurt me" thing from elementary school is the essence of this argument. What people say and do should not affect your thought process in the way that it affects your mood. Don't let other people's toxic traits, bad attitude, or shitty leadership dampen your motivation. Stay fixated on your goal as a leader.

Chapter 15

Right Plan – Wrong Executor

"When I find an employee who turns out to be wrong for the job, I feel it's my fault because I made the decision to hire him." – Akio Morita

Competence levels across the board are not equal between people. Everyone has their own strengths and weaknesses, and many times will not be able to execute the same plan the same way as someone else. This can be understood when watching the backup quarterback in an NFL game replace an injured starting quarterback. The game plan has to be adjusted to suit the capabilities of the new quarterback.

Having the right plan for any given situation is very useful if the person executing that plan knows how to coordinate and complete the plan. When you do not have the correct person chosen to complete a job, the task intricacies outweigh the competence level of that executor, making mission accomplishment much less likely.

If someone is not great at a task, it's probably best not to assign them to that task initially. This is not saying that developing that person is never to be considered, rather it is saying that when push comes to shove, it's best to have your top performer to complete the task. This top performer can train the other person to get better at the task and slowly relinquish control to the lower performer, but it should not start out as the lower performer's task.

If, after careful deliberation, a specific plan is selected, that plan needs to consider the intelligence and competence of the one who is overall tasked with it. For instance, let's say I am the CEO of a medium-sized consulting business specializing in C-suite leadership development. I have a client ask me to put on a seminar focused on small team dynamics. My choices to assign this task to are as follows: a newly hired, fresh-out-of-college intern who studied business operations and played quarterback in college, or a member of my team who served 20 years in a military unit within a small team and has been teaching classes on leadership and small team leadership for a decade.

The choice should be clear in this sense, but let's say we had to choose the quarterback. He may have some knowledge of the topic and will most likely be able to understand and regurgitate what he was taught in school. This is not a bad thing to be able to do, but what he is missing is the real-world experience that can provide substance to and support what was learned in college.

The right person for that job was obviously the 20-year small unit veteran. He has the knowledge and has applied the principles within a successful organization for over two decades. His experience, though not necessarily focused on business operations, is better suited to accomplish the class concerning small team dynamics.

Choose your executor deliberately. Don't just pick the next man up. This is not the NFL; the next man up may not be up to the task. Situations like this arise all the time in business when people are chosen based on fairness instead of quality. Don't choose the wrong person just because some arbitrary spreadsheet or garbage-ass guideline says so. Pick them based on merit.

Your plan might be the best one ever devised, or you might have picked the best play ever for your football game (maybe the Annexation of Puerto Rico. IYKYK), but if you pick the wrong person to execute it, you just lost. Be smart about where you assign people or what you ask of them. There might be better options on the table, and the wrong choice could make YOU expendable.

Chapter 16

Wrong Plan – Right Executor

"Selecting the right person for the right job is the largest part of coaching." – Phil Crosby

In this case, the executor's competence level outweighs the task intricacies, but the task is flawed and not the best option. The person completing or controlling the task understands this but makes the correct moves to get it done. It can almost be seen as someone shoving a square peg into a round hole with a mallet. You would not choose the gangly-looking person with zero upper body strength to do this task. You would choose the lumberjack-looking, corn-fed motherfucker to smash that peg into the hole.

This does not mean that literally anything can be completed using force (although this is often the case). What it means is that the right person leading a mission (even if it's flawed), the right person giving a briefing (even if the material is suspect), or the right person being given the ball on a bad play call are better options than waiting for the right plan and right executor to be available at the same time.

Many of us have had superiors shove horrible ideas or plans upon us that they expect to be completed successfully. This is very typical in the military, and the chain of command is usually at fault for this thought process. It's not ideal, but a lot can be learned, and it's the nature of being in the military.

Choose your top performer as the leader to force a plan to work or score a point even if the plan, idea, task, or play call was wrong. Be the mallet. Shove that square peg through the hole and make the plan work. The right executor can bring fantasy to reality if given just enough to do the job. These star performers have an uncanny ability to understand nearly any situation and make the right choices with little to no direct input. Seek them out and use them when the shit hits the fan, and there is no clear right choice in your plan or correct answer, especially if the plan is doomed to fail. They will surprise you.

Chapter 17

The Best Plan is Not the Perfect Plan

"A good plan, violently executed now, is better than a perfect plan next week." – George Patton

Much can be said about planning and how important it is to the execution of tasks within our everyday lives. Planning ensures all the things you want to do, all the people you want to be involved, and all the things you need to complete the task are synchronized and focused. Imagine trying to compete in a baseball game without each player knowing the rules, knowing their position, or having equipment available and a space to play in. Baseball, much like a combat mission, briefing, or class, does not spontaneously happen. A deliberate thought process goes into making ideas become reality, and this starts with planning.

There is a distinct difference between having the perfect and best plans. The perfect plan takes every single known variable into account and has an answer to all of them. This would be great if it weren't so impractical. These variables, hypothetical situations, and outside forces are never-ending, and one would have to continue planning and making plans inside of plans to accommodate all of them. Not only is this unrealistic, but it also creates a very complex situation.

The situation that was created by the perfect plan was too elaborate to control and had entirely too many moving pieces. This also leaves very little room for adaptability, where that very thing can make or break that mission, task, or briefing.

This "perfect plan" would be called the 100% plan, which simply does not work.

Instead, I would argue that a 75–80% plan executed violently is always the preferred method for accomplishing a mission. What does executing violently mean, you ask? It means that your conviction and confidence in the plan leaves nothing to the imagination, and "what if" questions never show their faces. You KNOW the plan is going to work because you planned appropriately and have absolute trust in your subordinates.

Now, this 75–80% plan is not going to be perfect, but it does take into consideration the time available and the competence of those executing the plan and allows for flexibility as the situation develops further. This is your best plan and the one you should choose. As a leader, it is up to you to know when the complexity of a plan is too much for you or your subordinates to handle.

We should strive for perfection but not to the extent where the juice is not worth the squeeze. Leave the door open for others to surprise you with their ingenuity. If you take too many precautions, you may miss the opening you had and may never have again. Make a good plan and execute it ruthlessly. Let the 75–80% plan turn into that 100% plan right before your eyes as you push through the breach with ferocity, determination, and grit.

Chapter 18

Make a Good First Impression, It's Your Only Shot

"If people are failing, they look inept. If people are succeeding, they look strong and good and competent. That's the 'halo effect.' Your first impression of a thing sets up your subsequent beliefs. If the company looks inept to you, you may assume everything else they do is inept." – Daniel Kahneman

Driving drunk is probably not a good first impression with the police. Not showering is probably not a good first impression for your date. Not knowing the material is probably not a good first impression for your upcoming meeting or sales pitch. First impressions are everyone's first and only chance to decide whether you are worthy of their time.

We interact with countless people throughout our lives. Some daily, some weekly, some just a few times in our lives, but one thing is certain…you cannot redo a first impression. No matter how hard you try, what people think when they first see, hear, or meet you for the first time will likely be their lasting impression of you. So, make it a strong one.

This goes for both leaders and subordinates. How your supervisor sees you initially might be the make-or-break point for your career. If you are late on the first day, unkempt, combative, inappropriate, etc., that may be their lasting impression of you, even if it was just a once-in-a-lifetime occurrence.

For the leader, if you come in guns blazing on your new team, they will immediately be taken aback and start questioning you, even if they don't come right out and say it. The first impression you make as a leader must instill motivation, pride, optimism, and respect. It should not be one that instills fear. Even though that does get results initially, it will not pan out in the long run and will eventually lead to a toxic environment within your team.

Let people see you for who you truly are right off the bat. If they know what to expect from you initially, there will be no learning curve, wrong impressions, or hesitation. Be an authentic leader. Let your words instill discipline, and let your actions show them. Make your first impression your best one, it's quite literally your only shot. Make it count.

Chapter 19

Second and Third Order Effects

"Failing to consider second- and third-order consequences is the cause of a lot of painfully bad decisions, and it is especially deadly when the first inferior option confirms your own biases. Never seize on the first available option, no matter how good it seems, before you've asked questions and explored." – Ray Dalio

What are second- and third-order effects, and why are they important?

An effect is something that happens as a result of something else. An example of this would be when you push the brake on a car, the car slows down. It's like a cause-and-effect situation that you learned about in elementary school.

A second-order effect would be the result of that initial effect being done. For instance, let's say you are running late for a very important meeting. You forgot to set your alarm and woke up late (first-order effect). Since you woke up late you missed your important meeting (second-order effect). Since you missed your meeting, your deputy had to give the pitch and couldn't close the deal (third-order effect).

In this scenario, and we could have kept it going with fourth, fifth, sixth etc., the results of our actions play into other areas that we did not anticipate. As a leader, this is not as simple as oops, I'll try again tomorrow. A leader must be able to analyze all situations and understand how their actions, or lack thereof, affect those around them. These second- and third-order effects can severely hamper any organization. This is why when you are tasked with something by a superior, it is advisable to get it done. That way, the monkey is now on their back.

Understanding that our actions have consequences really does ground you a little bit. Especially if you are a junior member of the organization. Learning is always happening, and no one can honestly say that they never made a mistake that either took someone else's time, made the mission fail, or had unanticipated consequences as a result.

As we talked about earlier, DYDJ! The second- and third-order effects often take more time to clean up than the initial effect. We get so caught up in only focusing on what matters to us in the present that we forget to look outward at how our actions affect others. Their time is valuable as well...maybe more than ours. It's best to finish what we start and finish it quickly and with attention to detail.

Chapter 20

Find Another Path…This Shit Ain't Working

"Insanity is doing the same thing over and over and expecting different results." – Albert Einstein

The quote sums up everything that we talked about. Doing the same shit repeatedly, thinking it will be different this time. Something has got to change. That might be your thought process, the inputs, your team, or how you approach the situation, but doing the same stuff day in and day out with little to no progress being made is wasteful and counterproductive. It's insane to think a different result will occur if we do not change any of the variables.

The Army has something called successive breaching. At its essence, it is a way to get into a locked area by using progressively more intense methods until you gain access. It starts with manual breaching (even though this is debated on whether it is one of the methods), which is basically just your hand or foot opening the door. This is followed by mechanical breaching, which is done via the use of a tool such as the trademark hooligan tool (hooly tool), sledgehammer, or something of that nature.

If the first ones do not work, you go to the ballistic breaches by using a weapon such as a shotgun to shoot out the material securing the deadbolt or hinges.

Next, we have explosive breaching, which is using some sort of explosive device such as a flex linear charge or a general purpose (GP) charge.

Finally, if all the other methods do not work, we have thermal breaching, which involves using a torch to melt or burn through the door, wall, or closed-off area.

As you can see, each of these is more violent than the next one. One way or another, if you tell a group of high-testosterone Rangers that you want to get into some room, you will get into that room.

Just as a Ranger would not keep using a hooligan tool to open a door that requires a GP charge, you should not keep attempting something that you know will not work. Think about it. Change some of the dynamics. Adjust your position. Get someone else's input. Do something different if nothing is working. You will be astonished to realize that some of the things you thought to be true were wrong, and that's why you were unsuccessful. It might have nothing to do with what you were wanting to do, but rather it may have something to do with how you are trying to do it.

There is no cookie-cutter solution for every problem you will face, but taking a step back and assessing the entire situation will give you a better perspective. Stop trying to force something to work if you have not changed any of the variables feeding it.

Chapter 21

Being Persistent and Being Dumb

"It is far better to grasp the universe as it really is than to persist in delusion, however satisfying and reassuring." – Carl Sagan

As a young man, I was energetic in nearly everything I did. Nothing seemed out of reach at the time, and I could make anything into a fun time. I could operate off only a couple of hours of sleep every night with very few issues. My body recovered quickly from the punishment I put it through. Like most young adult males, I was invincible.

Arguing and calling people idiots was a common refrain. I did not know when to quit things, often leading to my being lambasted by superiors and peers. I was a cocky little shit, to say the least. I had very little sense of "grounding" and had almost no understanding of how the real world worked even though I was old enough to fight in a war and old enough to buy cigarettes, old enough to take out loans with high interest, but not old enough to drink…though that issue was never really an issue ;-).

In late 2006, I was still assigned to the 3rd Ranger Battalion as a junior enlisted Soldier. Fresh off my second deployment, which was much more rigorous than the first, with a very high optempo (the pace at which different missions occur regarding the time available), I finally met the requirements to attend the US Army Ranger School after nearly a year of trying to get stronger. I had no idea how to do that and just assumed my youthful athletic ability would be enough to meet the minimum standard for my company to agree to send me (it wasn't), so I had to do a lot of pushups and sit-ups every night for a few weeks to get my muscles used to the fatigue.

I was sent to Ranger School for the first time soon after barely passing the Ranger Regiment pre-Ranger Course. I barely passed the initial PT test upon arrival to Ranger School after having to re-test pushups, but I was able to move on to the next few tests, all of which I passed…until I fucked up land navigation twice. Now, it's always up for debate on whether the instructors there would try to get you to quit, and it's warranted as they are breeding leaders there, but the whole dismissal from the course was shady in my eyes, though I take full responsibility for not being ready to go that time.

After returning to my unit, I was questioned by my chain of command, spoke to the Command Sergeant Major (a man that was known within the regiment for running barefoot for PT…IYKYK), and was sent packing to the First Infantry Division at Ft. Riley Kansas.

There would be no goodbye or thanks for your service, or hopefully, we will see you again. It was more or less: let's get this guy out of here so we can get another one in quickly to fill his role. I was no longer needed, and I did not live up to the Ranger Creed or standards required of the premier light infantry unit in the world. They did not have the time to get me ready to go back to school, and in their eyes, I was a quitter. Again, that's on me.

Upon arrival at the First Infantry Division, I was able to set myself apart from my peers very quickly and even made a bunch of new friends. I could easily complete most of the tasks assigned to me, given the tremendous amount of training I received from the top-notch leaders and Rangers with the Ranger regiment. I could run laps around most of the NCOs regarding small unit tactics and was instantly placed as a team leader. I believe I had more experience and knowledge about clearing rooms than anyone in my unit. This would be contested, proved, disproved, and proved several times again over.

We had deployed for the first time in 2008 to Camp Striker in Iraq. It was a fairly uneventful deployment for my company, but our battalion suffered a few casualties from an improvised explosive device. After a year, we returned and began our ramp-up for our next deployment in about a year. In the middle of that train-up, I was selected to return to Ranger School after getting myself in a lot better shape. Even though I had a crappy Company Commander this time who reluctantly signed off on my packet, I was still returning to Ranger School to squash the demons from my time in the Ranger regiment and get my black and gold Ranger tab.

I arrived at Ranger School in the best shape I had ever been in. I easily passed the PT test and all other events…land navigation included. I was cruising through the initial assessments until the ruck march came up. It was a shitty weather forecast that August, and we were in the 90s with 100% humidity, even at 0300 in the morning. I had just gotten over a stomach bug the week before flying to Georgia, and even though I thought I was fine, that turned out to be false.

I got through the first 10-ish miles through grit and determination, calling up to God several times to get me through to the next checkpoint. The last thing I recall was some guys telling me to stop and give my ruck to the medic. I have sporadic memories of having my core temperature checked (IYKYK) and sporadic memories about what my temperature was: someone said 104, and someone said 101. Either way, I could not complete the ruck march or the Ranger course at that time either. I left with my tail between my legs again, this time without being allowed to stay.

I have had other opportunities to return to Ranger School in my career, but I have declined the option each time. My priorities have changed, and there were other ways to get to the level of being a great leader other than always trying to persist with going back and forth. This is not to say that Ranger School or striving for excellence are not great qualities, rather they are not the only redeeming qualities that a person can have. We forget that a lot in the military; leaders also need to understand that. Sadly, many do not.

Persistence is only good if the results have not wasted so many other opportunities that you may have had. I may not have gotten married, met some of my closest friends, or learned so much about myself if I decided to continue trying to get my Ranger tab. You need to understand when it is time to move on from what you once thought you wanted to another objective. Stop being dumb and hardheaded. Not everyone has the same mindset, and you can be just as successful by changing yours.

Chapter 22

Learning From Bad Leaders and Toxic Ones

"A bad leader can take a good staff and destroy it, causing the best employees to flee and the remainder to lose all motivation." – Unknown

Bad leaders and toxic leaders are not the same thing, even though some leaders fall into both categories. You may have a bad leader who is not a toxic one and a toxic one who is not necessarily a bad one. But first, let's define what we're talking about when we say bad and toxic leaders.

Bad leaders are ones that are just not up to the standard to which they should be. They may have a flaw in their knowledge, personality, fitness, or decision-making. They may mean well in the grand scheme of things, but being able to make things happen is kind of important as a leader. These leaders are not necessarily bad people; they do not have all the qualities needed in their current position, or if they do have them, they are not tuned finely enough. Remedial or additional training, schooling, or mentoring would probably be appropriate for these people.

A toxic leader is one who abuses their power as a way of getting what they want. They have none or very minimal empathy for others and do not generally care about how their actions affect others. They are strictly focused on covering their own ass on the backs of their subordinates. They may put up a façade like they care, but in reality they are scheming about how to create an advantage, feigning compassion or care, or figuring out how to make it someone else's problem.

These leaders are a very common fixture of military life, but they mostly weed themselves out after a while...mostly. Usually, the best practice is to compartmentalize your team and do your best as a leader to shield them from the BS that that person brings.

When I served as a senior leader in a specialized unit, we had the distinct "pleasure" of having a leader as our unit Commander who was completely full of himself and seemed to only care about looking good to his superiors, or that's how it seemed to most of the unit. His policies were atrocious, and how he interacted with everyone was borderline condescending and hateful. It got to its breaking point as my Commander and I neared the end of our tenure in the unit, when one of our Soldiers did his job perfectly, only to have the aforementioned Commander punish him because it made him look bad.

This Soldier was one of the most highly trained in the unit and went through a rigorous selection and training program before being allowed to conduct his duties in view of the public. So, when the incident happened, which I witnessed first-hand, my Soldier did exactly what he was trained to do in that situation. The unit Commander did not see it that way, and by trying to cite "diplomatic relations" and downplaying the ignorance of both our higher unit and the foreign personnel involved in the situation, he came across as a very arrogant, smug, smarter-than-everyone-in-the-room-boss whose ambition was more important than standing up for his Soldiers.

When he brought my Commander and I, along with our Commander and select staff into a meeting, which was more of a verbal assault on our leadership and him demanding we had to earn his trust again, I had lost the remainder of respect for this man and vowed never to be that type of leader. He apparently did not like it when someone told him he was wrong and that I believed our Soldier did the right thing and his boss's team was to blame for the whole fiasco, as he abruptly left. My Commander and I changed out of our positions soon after that, but the impression that this "hand-picked" senior Army leader had left on me, and seemingly the entire unit, was depressing, to say the least.

I learned from that specific incident that speaking up requires tact and knowledge of the overall impact of the entire situation. Not everything requires a fight, but when you are in a position of trust, you must speak up when the situation requires it. Your subordinates need it, and sometimes your peers and superiors need to know that you will tell them the hard truths that they need to hear.

Our careers are filled with issues such as this, albeit more nuanced and appropriate to our own situations. Learning what works and doesn't work in any given situation requires a certain skill set that cannot be found in books. It requires experience that can only be found by making bad decisions or observing others.

I do not have hard feelings for this leader as I do feel he learned just as much from that interaction as I did, but situations like that make trust in leadership very hard for junior leaders to have. Be willing to hear arguments no matter who they are from. You may not have the best grasp on the entirety of the situation.

Chapter 23

Learning from Peers and Learning for Yourself

"Learn from the mistakes of others. You can't live long enough to make them all yourself." – Eleanor Roosevelt

Let the path others make give you guidance for your own choices. There is no reason to reinvent the wheel. Why must we always try to make our mark on the world? Why can't leaders just accept that the way things were done before their arrival was actually a good way to do things? There is no reason to always change things, especially if the person you are using as an example was doing a pretty good job. Your mark does not have to be a personal one. Being a steward is just as valuable as making your mark.

Learning from yourself is another aspect that any leader must practice. Knowing what not to do. Knowing what failed them in the past and knowing what worked in the past. Knowing when to push and when to pull. The experiences that fill up the career of any leader are all things that they must learn and grow from, both good and bad.

Learning from others' mistakes and good ideas and learning from your own mistakes and good ideas make transitioning into a new position much easier. There's no need to do something if you know it won't work. Many things that you are going to try have already been tried before. Seek that information out. Find out what went right or wrong and see if you should try doing it or scrap it.

When I first got placed into a leadership position, I had learned from the best in the Ranger Battalion. They taught me everything about small unit tactics and what it was to be an infantryman. I used what they had taught me and imparted that knowledge to my first fire team. We did well during our first few training events and live fire events. I didn't try to reinvent a new way to do battle drill six or a new way to patrol. I used proven techniques and implemented them ferociously.

I learned a lot from others who had been doing the same job as me for years. Their interactions with their teams, squads, platoons, and companies and how they conducted training were all useful to me as a junior and now senior leader. I learned how to maximize my time with my Soldiers while also ensuring the behind-the-scenes paperwork was completed on time. I learned things about tactics that I never learned in my career from people who were in the same job as me but had a different career path to get where they were. Learn all you can from everyone you can.

That's what being a leader is all about. Knowing what works and implementing it with violence of action, ferocity, and attention to detail. Don't think that you won't be noticed if you don't change things. People will see how effective and efficient you are by not wasting time and changing things that don't need to be changed. Conserve your time and energy. Focus on the things that matter. Your own pride is not what matters. The job being accomplished does.

Chapter 24

"Do as I Say, Not as I do" is Necessary at Times

"Sometimes a hypocrite is nothing more than a man in the process of changing." – Brandon Sanderson

There is a saying that goes, "Do as I say, not as I do." Another saying goes, "Practice what you preach." Both idioms are getting to a very similar point: do yourself what you are telling others to do. This sounds great in theory and is a solid idea for one to get behind. However, there is something to be said about not always having to practice what you preach. Sure, it might not seem morally good to have others do something that you yourself are not doing, but there are occasions when it may be necessary.

Examples of this can be found all over. One such example would be a smoker telling others not to smoke. Another would be when you tell your children to drive the speed limit when they are just learning to drive, knowing full well that you yourself speed all the time…YES, even five miles per hour over is still speeding.

There are other examples of this where people who cannot control their behavior don't want others to follow in their footsteps. The issues surrounding this could be morality, ethics, or even safety-focused but just because someone is not doing themselves what they tell you to do, does not mean that their advice is flawed. They may know that their vices are too powerful for them to overcome at that moment.

Take any advice given with a balanced view without letting your preconceived ideas cloud your judgment. Even immoral, vile people can have good advice and a keen eye for things; in fact, their view may be more in tune with what is wrong. They may even be able to have more clarity in that type of situation since that is something that has plagued them for some time.

As a leader, this is something that you will hear all the time, and you should try your best to practice what you preach. However, it is not a hard rule but more of a guideline. Do as I say, not as I do, is sometimes necessary. One's own demons may prevent them from doing what they are telling you to do. If you are the one being advised, don't try to find the flaw in the argument and play the "gotcha" game with them. If their advice makes sense and aims to improve you, no matter how they carry themselves, take the instruction. Even people with bad leadership traits can provide redeeming advice at times. Understand when it is the latter and execute.

Chapter 25

Make Incremental Changes...Don't Upend the Whole Ship

"Great things are not done by impulse, but by a series of small things brought together." – Vincent Van Gogh

When you initially arrive at your next assignment or get brought into a new position, possibly promoted, as a leader you are entrusted to not only be a steward for that organization but to also improve the organization. There is a fine line between the two of these. On one hand, you need to ensure the organization will continue its mission well into the future just as it has done before your arrival. On the other hand, you are charged with improving the organization to help it reach new heights.

The issues arise when you begin making too many changes too soon in your tenure. Sure, some organizations or businesses require it, but a good rule of thumb is to not change the whole dynamic of the unit or organization right off the bat. Doing so will make others resent you personally and as a leader. Having people resent you and having peers despise you is a recipe for disaster.

You may have to make a few quick changes, especially if you are on a strict timeline, but those quick changes should be explained well to those it affects. Providing your vision or philosophy and your motivation for making those changes should help to alleviate some concern and pushback...some, not all.

As you continue your first few months of learning about the organization and who the key players are, what they bring to the table, and knock out a SWOT analysis (strengths, weaknesses, opportunities, threats) of your organization, it would be advisable to do a rough draft of things that you notice that may need tweaking for the future. This does not mean that you should start making those things happen immediately, rather you should simply take note of them or write them down and anything that could cause problems should you decide to implement those changes.

If you decide to upend the whole ship right off the bat, even though some organizations need this, you could unintentionally accelerate the regression or stagnation that's happening with that business or organization.

I have only made a couple of immediate changes upon arrival for each new position I have been assigned to, especially those in leadership facets. These changes were to create some familiarity for myself immediately within the organization and create an easier process for those relying on me. As time went on, I would slowly add more changes to the unit, which were usually subtle enough not to cause many issues but which made the organization run smoother.

Each military unit, business, and organization are unique in their needs, but very few organizations successfully change what had made them successful to begin with. Make incremental changes. Your ship doesn't need to be sunk if it's heading in the right direction. Who knows, the ship may make you a humbler person and help you reach new heights.

Chapter 26

Situational Awareness

"I am a Federal Air Marshal. That's the career path I chose, and for the past nineteen years, I've had a first-class ticket into the world of covert surveillance, surveillance detection, and self-defense. If I had to access all the training I've received throughout my career and pick one essential skill I could pass along to everyone I care about, it would be situational awareness." – Gary Quesenberry

You must always know where you are, including who you are around and what the current environment is. This is called situational awareness and it is one of the hardest things to instill among new leaders. Sometimes, it is a skill that people are born with, but often, it's something that needs a lot of work.

You don't need just to know where you are physically located, rather you need to know where you are, who is there currently, and who could potentially be there in the future. What happened, what is happening, and what is probably going to happen are also some things that play into situational awareness. What matters to you as the leader may not matter much to your team, so it's best to remind them to remain situationally aware.

This goes for all aspects of the job at hand. You need to know who is around you when inside a room or when you are about to give out some information. Do the people around need to be there for it? Are they ear-hustling for info, or are they just in the wrong place? In a combat zone, you need to know where your Soldiers are at all times. This is to protect you from fratricide. You must also know where the enemy is located or where they could be located both now and in the future.

Maintaining situational awareness on the job site, such as on a construction site, on a fishing boat, or in the cockpit of an airplane, requires a keen sense of knowing what to do and knowing what matters at that moment. If you lose focus for just a second or two, that could be a missed chance, an injured co-worker, or a lost checkpoint.

As a leader, before pushing out sensitive information I had to ensure that only the people with a need-to-know were actually within earshot. This was done to protect those who were affected by our meetings and to protect the command from any liability. Take ownership of privileged information, and don't let it fall into the wrong hands, no matter how innocent it may seem.

As the leader, people trust you to always remain professional and to maintain their dignity; don't give them a reason to doubt your values by not doing what you're supposed to be doing.

Being charged with leadership of any sort is an immense honor and should never be taken lightly. Don't let a rumor spread, your mission become compromised, or your friend become embarrassed by a decision you made, or a miscalculation of someone else's intentions. Have your wits about you and keep the wolf out of the hen house.

Chapter 25

Letter of the Law vs. Spirit of the Law

"Useless laws weaken the necessary laws." –
Charles-Louis De Secondat Montesquieu

Everything has a reason for existing. Stoplights are there for a reason. Laws are enforced for a reason. Regulations are put into place for a reason. The list goes on, but the fact of the matter is, everything has a reason why it was created, and people have reasons for why they do things.

The letter of the law is the black-and-white, no-gray-area type of enforcing something that is written. For instance, if you intentionally kill someone, that's murder. It's black and white. There is no real argument if all you know is that someone killed someone else. The letter of the law would be to punish them for that. However, if you consider that the person who was killed was trying to harm someone else and that someone was trying to stop them, then it becomes a little less black and white. It's more of a gray area here. The letter of the law says to punish the person who killed the other person, but the spirit of the law says that the "killer" was justified in what he did.

So, what should you do then? You need to understand what a certain law, regulation, directive, or order is trying to communicate. Not everything will fall into a black-and-white, yes, or no, right, or wrong area. There are situations that require a subjective approach by the leader.

If someone is late to work, the letter of the law might be to reprimand them. But think about why that guideline was put into place. Is it in place to punish everyone or just those who consistently show that they can't arrive on time?

If a piece of paperwork has some grammatical errors but can still be clearly understood, does it make sense to send it back to the originator since that's what your job says to do? Or does it make more sense not to waste time and get it processed? That regulation is probably more focused on ensuring the document or paperwork communicates what the sender wanted it to communicate. I understand that some jobs need to be as close to perfect as possible with their paperwork, but there is also some room to save time and money by ignoring small, non-important errors.

There are countless other examples we could use to describe the differences and nuances concerning the letter of the law and the spirit of the law, each focused on a different job or duty. The job of a boss, leader, supervisor, or reviewer is to understand that these two items are different. They must know when it is appropriate to ignore the letter of the law and when it is appropriate to apply a spirit of the law concept. Jumping to conclusions when in a position of influence is never a smart idea, even if you think you know all the intricacies involved.

Take a breath, think about the variables of the situation, and then decide. Don't rush to judgment because others are clamoring for it. Don't rush to judgment because your shareholders are out for blood. You are in that position for a reason, so earn it.

Chapter 28

Leading Without Being the Leader

"Basically, to lead without a title is to derive your power within the organization not from your position but from your competence, effectiveness, relationships, excellence, innovation and ethics" – Robin S. Sharma

In the military, there is a disparity between the officer corps and the enlisted service members. The officers are charged with leading and creating plans to accomplish missions. The enlisted or, more accurately, the noncommissioned officers, are the ones who take that plan and make it come to fruition in accordance with the officers' vision. These two drastically different yet mutually supporting jobs both have a purpose, and both are very much needed in the military. An argument can be made that these two job types mirror the civilian workforce as well, with the officers being managers and the enlisted being the everyday employee.

As a senior noncommissioned officer, I have had the privilege of influencing officers, junior NCOs, and lower enlisted. While on paper, I am not the guy who makes the final decision, I do provide my insight for all matters that concern the leader (officer). This can include anything from planning and personnel issues to budgetary and training issues. Granted, I have never been and will never be THE leader, but being able to influence and set an example to the rest of the formation or organization, in a sense, makes me a leader as well.

As the right-hand man of the officer, an NCO is the person with whom that officer can confide, bounce ideas off, and have in their corner when they make the final decision. Disagreements always arise regarding the choices that are made, but they should always happen behind closed doors. Once those doors are opened, a united front is necessary.

Being the leader while being led (we will call this person the led leader) is typically the role of middle management or, more simply, everyone that falls between the CEO and the lowest person on the totem pole. The led leader can influence the leader with their insight and guidance and can also influence their subordinates by supporting the leader's decisions.

So, how can you lead while being led? Simple.

- Be on time
- Be what you want your personnel to be
- Speak up when necessary
- Turn in a good product
- Ask when you do not understand or need help
- Go out of your way to help others
- Help others even if there is nothing in it for you

I think you get the point.

You are still an important piece of the machine, even if you are not the one making the decisions. You are still a leader, even if your name is not on the door. Supervisors are leaders. Foremen are leaders. Senior employees are leaders. Men are leaders. Women are leaders. Everyone is a leader, and they show it by their actions and by being a reliable, morally stout person. Don't think that just because you are not the one signing the checks that your actions do not hold credence with others, because they absolutely do.

Chapter 29

Don't Take Things Personal

"Not taking things personally is a true sign of maturity." - Robert Celner

Get your stupid ass emotions out of your decision-making or your reactions to a decision that was made. Stop taking things personally.

In the military, just as in business, decisions are made countless times throughout the day, each affecting the overall success of that organization. Everything, in theory, should run more efficiently when emotions are taken out of the mix. Emotional decision-making or reactions to decisions that have been made show a lack of control of oneself.

I have been in many leadership positions and positions of influence in the military during my career. I have had the privilege of leading Soldiers in combat and training the next generation of both enlisted service members as a drill sergeant and officers as an ROTC instructor. In my time, I have had many disagreements, verbal altercations, and physical altercations occur that all stemmed from taking things too personally.

As a senior advisor to the Commander, my advice to them was usually heard, making me feel great. When I was not heard, or felt that they did not listen or had already made up their mind, it pissed me off since I felt like it wasted my time.

It can be hard to come to terms with one's voice not being heard when speaking up or when a disagreement occurs, but this is natural. We all need to feel important, and when someone seemingly slights us, whether intentionally or unintentionally, it can drive us mad and affect us for the rest of the day, week, or even years in the future.

Once you understand this, you can nip it in the bud much more easily and continue with your day. Not everything we do, say, or recommend needs to be accepted by others. Our actions may not affect them the way we intended, and their actions may not affect us the way they intended. IT IS OK. Have your disagreements, professionally and behind closed doors, come up with a plan and execute that plan. Your personal feelings do not mean shit in the grand scheme. It is just business. If you cannot be trusted to take your own feelings and emotions out of the arrangement, you should probably re-evaluate yourself.

Be rational, hear what others have to say, and stop wearing your emotions on your sleeve...especially when in a position of influence. People look to you for guidance, and you cannot provide that to them if you are affected by every little action that others take. On the flip side, if you are a subordinate, don't take what your superiors do as a knock at you, even if it is. Don't let them see it affecting you. Be a cold-hearted SOB that doesn't let little things sway you from being a good worker into a shitbag. Their decisions were most likely not meant to be personal, either.

Chapter 30

Say What You Mean and Mean What You Say

"Say what you mean and mean what you say." – George Patton

Don't beat around the bush. If you have something to say, say it. If you don't mean it, then shut the hell up. As a leader, you must be able to follow through with what you are saying. Words do not mean anything if the repercussions are slim to nil. Leaders must hold people accountable for their actions and themselves as well. Although this book supports the fact that a "do as I say, not as I do" philosophy is sometimes needed, great leaders walk the walk and talk the talk.

Don't use too many analogies or big words to sound smart or flex your educational muscles. Use common words so everyone can understand what you are saying. If some in your organization do not understand what you are talking about, that's a flaw on your part as the leader. You need to understand your audience. If they don't know what you want, how can you expect them to tell their subordinates what you want? Answer...YOU CAN'T.

If you tell your team that you will be coming to inspect their paperwork at 1 p.m. on Thursday, inspect it at 1 p.m. on Thursday.

If you give a class and provide the information for the quiz or test that needs to be studied, that's what you need to quiz or test them on.

If you tell your kids that you will take them to the park later, go there later that same day. Kids don't have a firm grasp on what later means, they attribute it to later that day.

Likewise, if you tell your friends you will be at a place later or will arrive at a certain time, stick to that timeline.

If you tell your boss you will have the paperwork done by a certain time, have it done by that time. Don't be optimistic or pessimistic, be realistic (more on this later).

Everything we say and do reflects our character. You may only interact with someone a few times, so make those interactions accurate (notice I did not say positive). Let others know what they can expect when dealing with you. Don't threaten to take a specific action if you do not intend to follow through. Actually mean what you say. Your words need to have teeth. Your subordinates, peers, and superiors must know that if you say something, it is calculated, and you will make it happen.

Chapter 31

Effectiveness vs. Efficiency

"Efficiency is doing things right; effectiveness is doing the right things." – Peter Drucker

Effectiveness is defined as the degree to which something is successful in producing a desired result. This does not consider the supplies, manpower, or other inputs to accomplish that particular job, task, or work. It's basically how well the job itself was done. An example of effectiveness would be an artillery barrage completely obliterating one enemy tank.

Efficiency is defined as achieving maximum productivity with minimum wasted effort or expense. An example of efficiency would be that same artillery barrage taking out an entire tank platoon or a single artillery round taking out a singular tank. In other words, this is getting the best bang for your buck, whereas effectiveness is just getting the job done correctly. Efficiency considers how much it took to get that result. Both metrics can help a leader see what their organization values.

Resources are finite for most organizations, meaning they will eventually run out. Manpower, printer ink, paper, work hours etc. Anything can be seen as a resource that needs to be tracked. When a leader is given a job to get done, they need to know what resources they have at hand and how much time they have allotted to complete that job. These two things will tell them whether they need to be effective or efficient. You can start off in either category and transition towards the other as the situation develops.

If the assignment is time-sensitive, it might be beneficial to start with a more effectiveness-focused mindset. Get the job done. This ensures deadlines are met and time is saved. If the assignment requires close monitoring of supply utilization, starting with an efficiency-focused mindset is probably best.

An organization can be effective and efficient, but this would not necessarily be the norm. Know what your organization values, and you can make the correct choice. If money is an issue, be more efficient. If money is not an issue, be effective.

In the grand scheme of things, getting the job done is at the heart of business and being a leader. Once this can be done easily, you can then start trying to be more efficient with your time, supplies, money, and personnel.

Be effective first, then learn to be efficient.

Chapter 32

The 4 C's of Leaders (Competence – Confidence – Conviction – Care)

"A true leader has the confidence to stand alone, the courage to make tough decisions, and the compassion to listen to the needs of others. He does not set out to be a leader, but becomes one by the equality of his actions and the integrity of his intent." – Douglas MacArthur

We have already talked about what the definition of leadership is. Now we will discuss the parts that make leaders effective and worthy of following. These characteristics, which are very similar to what General MacArthur was talking about in the above quote, are known as the 4 Cs of leadership and are a blueprint for success in the military, corporate world, in your personal life, or anything else that requires a leader's guidance or mentoring. The 4 Cs are competence, confidence, conviction, and care.

Competence is knowing one's job and all that it entails. It is the baseline for becoming a leader. You cannot be one if you do not know how to do what you must do. For instance, a pilot must have a pilot's license, a doctor must have passed medical school, and a Soldier must have passed basic training or something of that sort. Many other professions have baseline requirements as well, but this does not mean you are competent. You must know the nuances that play into your job or specialty.

For example, a pilot with a PPL does not have the knowledge to fly a Boeing 747 or a space shuttle properly. Sure, they may understand aerodynamics and aircraft flight characteristics, but they do not know how each decision they make will affect the flight of that airframe. They need additional training and experience to do these jobs properly.

A Soldier does not simply get thrust into a command position without having attended the appropriate schools or completing the prescribed training. Sure, there are always outliers that buck the typical trend but, for the most part, military leaders have all been trained to understand their jobs. I would not expect a basic Soldier to be able to shoot a target as well as a trained sniper. That sniper has had years of training and has been to courses and shot many rounds to get to the point that they are now at. Becoming competent in layman's terms means you must know what is expected at your current position, and understand every aspect of the job you are in, or at least know how to find the answer that's needed.

Confidence is trusting what you know and being able to project that to your subordinates. You know what you know and know what you don't know and by understanding your limitations you become more aware of your decision making. Trust in oneself and one's abilities will emanate from within. Confidence comes from within too. It is hard to come by if you do not have the competence required for your position. It takes effort to be competent but once you get to the point where your understanding of your job is peerless, the confidence will start to develop easier and easier. This does take work but it's not something that is unattainable. Keep chugging along and get yourself out there. Show what you know. You'll be surprised that you are seen as an expert in your field just by exuding confidence in what you are saying.

There are several definitions of the word "conviction" but the one we are focused on is "the quality of showing that one is firmly convinced of what one believes or says." This idea means that YOU actually believe what you are saying and will follow it through to fruition. Nothing can prevent you from accomplishing your goal. This aspect of the 4 C's builds upon the previous two. For competence, knowing your job is key. For confidence, your trust in your knowledge is key. Now for conviction, your dedication to your objective is key.

Maintaining conviction or one's credo is one of the most important aspects of being a leader. You must keep your plane flying, your ship afloat, your business churning while the highs and lows of the world descend upon you. This is not something everyone can do. We are constantly bombarded by outside forces, each with their own agenda, but a leader recognizes this and brushes them off, keeping their eye on the goal. They remain dedicated to their plan through thick and thin. This does not mean that they are not open to advice but rather that they have an end state in mind and that should not be disturbed. The way to it can change with new knowledge, but the task remains the same.

Finally, as a leader, you must care. Care about how your decisions impact others. Care about the future of the company. Care about the second- and third- order effects of your decisions. Anything a leader does will have an impact on the future of their business, unit, or home life. This must be considered and if one does not display empathy when making decisions, it will inevitably come back on them.

Now, all these characteristics of a leader should be applied in that order to get to your desired results. You must know your job (competence), trust in your knowledge (confidence), remain true to your goals (conviction), and have empathy for those who are affected by your decisions (care). Apply the 4 Cs in your life and you'll be shocked at how much more you can accomplish.

Chapter 33

Message Sent Does Not Mean Message Received

"The message sent is not always the message received." – Virginia Smith

Email, text messages, and second-hand communication, such as someone telling you what another person said, are crap. You lose context, substance, and meaning with these mediums. We tend to lose sight of this and believe that all mediums project the same type of message. Sadly, this is not the case, nor has it ever been. The more disconnected the source is from the receiver, the more convoluted the message received will be.

One cannot place proper emphasis on certain aspects of an email the same as you could in person. Quotation marks are not good enough. Bold font is not good enough. If you think it is, YOU are not good enough.

What I believe to be true, another person may not. What I want the focus to be, another person may not. These two reasons are why it is vital for leaders of all types to not only put out detailed guidance but to also have the guidance briefed back to them to ensure understanding and answer any pertinent questions. This is called back briefing, and it is a way to ensure that what was sent is the same as what was received.

In the military we use something called a PACE plan. It is an acronym that stands for Primary, Alternate, Contingency, and Emergency. It is used primarily for communication during missions and provides a method to maintain contact with all personnel during the entirety of the operation. This way, the Commander can provide guidance and receive updates quickly and on schedule.

In the business setting it is advisable (albeit with exceptions based upon job type and accessibility) to use the following types of communication in order: In-person, Videocall (Facetime, Skype etc.), Phone Call, Text Message, Email, Message, Messenger (another person). As you can see, they start at face-to-face contact and steadily move toward more distant approaches. The more detailed a plan must be, the more direct the form of communication should be.

In addition to using this PACE plan, it might also be a great idea to follow up with an alternate method of communication to further reinforce the primary form that was used. All these techniques and mediums are focused on one singular point...ensuring the message you wanted to send out is the same message that was received.

It is convenient to send a text message or fire and forget with an email, but the fact of the matter is that your message may not be the one the intended recipient understands.

Part of your charge as a leader and subordinate is ensuring you understand the message as it was intended and that your message is understood by the receiver as intended. MAKE THE DAMN PHONE CALL or TALK TO THEM

IN PERSON. Get your point across so there is no misunderstanding. If you don't, then you can't blame them for not understanding.

Chapter 34

Do Whatever Your Constitution Can Handle

"If you can't handle stress, you won't manage success." – Sushant Singh

If you don't want to find out, it's best not to fuck around. More on this statement later.

As a leader in any organization, especially those in which you have someone higher than you to report to, you have a lot at stake for every decision you make. Your choices show others what you care about and inform others of your future intentions. If you can't handle the consequences of your actions or you cannot take all the punishment that comes with being the leader, you are in the wrong line of work.

Doing whatever your constitution can handle means that you do not habitually cross the bounds of which you are willing to fight. It's that invisible line that exists after you have made a decision and the point at which once crossed, there is no turning back. It's not clear and you might not know when that line is crossed but you better anticipate it and be ready for the repercussions, some of which might be severe.

If you can't stomach the attacks that are to come or if you can't push through the negativity that follows, it is going to be a damn near impossible task getting others to follow you or do as you command. You are the one who all others gain their momentum and motivation from. If you are not committed to the cause, prepared for the outcomes, and are not able to keep yourself mentally and physically present to guide your organization, you should not be in charge.

If you are not prepared to commit yourself to the mission, remove yourself from the equation. Let the next man up do it. After all, that's why you are in charge right? To accomplish the mission assigned to you. This does not apply to those just in military or law enforcement, it applies to those in any facet of leadership within business, sports, and education as well.

The whole fuck around and find out adage is harsh language but the insight gathered from those four words hits the point of our internal constitution. Cut through the BS, take an internal look at yourself, and make the right choice. Then stick by it. And remember, if you don't want to find out, it's best not to fuck around.

Chapter 35

Fight Smart. You Can't Hit All Targets at Once

"The shortest way to do many things is to do only one thing at a time." – Mozart

Have you ever been on a rifle qualification range? I have. The one in particular I am talking about is the Army rifle qualification range with targets that go from 50 meters out to 300 meters, and every 50 meters in between. You are given three magazines, two with 10 rounds and one with 20 rounds. You will fire from the prone supported (laying down with some type of support to steady your weapon), prone unsupported (laying down without a support for your weapon), and kneeling firing positions...of course now the qualification standard has changed but the essence is still there.

You need to hit 23 out of 40 targets to be considered "qualified" and remain in good standing (or "current" to all you military folk). It's a basic standard and not hard to do. In fact, most people can do it with fewer than two magazines.

The targets come up either one at a time or two at a time in a set interval and for only a few seconds. The proper way to engage these targets is to shoot the nearest target first and then the farther one. This ensures you take out the closest threat to you first and instills this same thinking in combat situations. The thinking is that in a real-life scenario, that target could be an enemy who has an easier shot at you since he is closer so it is in your best interest to take him out quickly.

To engage the target, you must be able to maintain a steady firing position, aim your rifle properly, control your breathing, and pull on the trigger slowly with the sights still on the target. This is something that you must pass in basic training to even become a Soldier. It becomes easier the more you do it and before you know if you will be able to qualify easily.

As these targets pop up, you must identify them quickly and apply the fundamentals in quick succession and then hit your target before transitioning to the next one. It can be stressful but it can also be managed by proper coaching.

If all the targets on the range decided to pop up at one time, you would have no chance of being able to hit them all before they go down. Your best bet is to try hitting the biggest threats first, your 50-meter and 100-meter targets. There's no reason to engage the farther targets without taking out the ones that will affect you sooner.

If you are always trying to take on a ton of tasks at once, you will never be successful. Sure, you may be able to accomplish some of them but without focusing on a select few tasks, the result will be garbage. Pick and choose where you focus your energy. A broad look at many topics is not as effective as a concentrated look at a couple important ones. You will run out of ammo (energy / supplies) before you complete all of them.

Fight smarter!

Chapter 36

Don't Be Optimistic or Pessimistic, Just Be Realistic

"The pessimist complains about the wind. The optimist expects it to change. The leader adjusts the sails." – John C. Maxwell

A quick Google search will tell you that optimism means to have a hopefulness and confidence about the future. You feel good about your chances of winning or making things right. You have considered all aspects of the situation and more than a half of the results point towards you being victorious. It's a great feeling to have. Optimism.

Pessimism, as a quick search tells us, means seeing the worst aspect of things or believing the worst is going to happen. Just like optimism, you have calculated all the inputs and more than half point towards defeat. This is not a great feeling to have nor to have people surround you that think like this.

While both are the extremes for how we feel about our chances, they are not what you should focus on. I'd suggest being realistic instead. This means taking all the inputs and applying a decision-making process and coming to a conclusion that is grounded in reality. False optimism or wanting something to happen, even though it might make you feel good, will most likely have you reeling in self-pity when the goal you were planning on doesn't come to fruition.

Likewise, pessimism about everything can have the same result but will also reinforce an incorrect view on the future since you always believe you're going to fail. If this is your mentality, you need to re-examine your choices. You may need to prepare yourself better or maybe even change your career path. Maybe surround yourself with people who are more optimistic than yourself. Either way, a completely pessimistic attitude is a negative one that needs to be stopped in its tracks.

A realistic attitude towards life and your plan will help with staying grounded and making informed decisions. While optimism seems to breed emotion, remaining realistic about one's chances of success makes sense for everyone.

When a superior asks about the likeness of something occurring, don't feed them optimistic BS. Tell them the truth, they need to hear it. Don't feed them pessimistic BS either since that will cause them to question your motives. Be realistic when you are giving them information. They need correct data to make that informed decision and keep the organization moving. Feelgood data (optimism) needs to be kept away from the decision-making process.

Be smart with how you articulate yourself to others as an overabundance of both optimism and pessimism will affect how others think of you, treat you, and respect you.

Chapter 37

Cut Sling-Load / Slip Away / Break Contact

"My past has not defined me, destroyed me, deterred me, or defeated me; it has only strengthened me." – Steve Maraboli

People are toxic.

Not all people, but you should take this thought process into every interaction you have with others. Let them show you what they are all about, what their intrinsic motivators are, what they value, what their morals and beliefs are. These things are all indicators that can tell you when it's time to cut sling-load, slip away, or break contact. These terms are used in the military to describe when it's time to stop what you're doing, get out of a situation, or cease talking to someone.

Cut sling-load is a term that describes when a helicopter is used as a transporter for some equipment or supplies. Said equipment or supplies are attached to the undercarriage of the aircraft via a rope (granted its thick as hell) and lifted and transported to its destination. If the conditions while flying with that sling-load turn dangerous, it's at the pilot's discretion whether to cut sling-load, or jettison that load for the safety of the pilot and aircraft. The military uses it to describe when it's time to leave an awkward situation or something of that nature.

Slip away is a term used to avoid a situation or leave any situation before it becomes an issue. The term slip away is used by paratroopers when descending from the aircraft under their parachutes. As they near another paratrooper or see that they are about to hit something dangerous to their health, they "slip away" by pulling on the parachute risers (the straps that attach the parachute itself to the paratroopers themselves), to change the direction of their descent or travel.

Break contact is a term that describes both a military battle drill where you are under enemy fire and have to "retreat," for lack of a better term, and regroup. It is also a term that means to get out of an interaction or conversation with someone that is either awkward, dangerous, or not advantageous.

All three of these terms can be applied to your daily interactions with everyone. If you realize that your planned meeting is going to be a waste of time or your sales pitch is going to be less effective than you hoped, cut sling load. Cut your losses and try again at a later time. Don't try to force it into a dangerous situation. If you are in a conversation that you believe is going the wrong way and you may slip up and say something stupid, break contact or slip away. This is one of those times when it's good to have a confidant who realizes the situation you are in and can bail you out. This is also a great thing for blind dates if you don't feel safe or if you are not meshing.

These terms can also be applied to individual people with whom you have had close relationships with. They might be bad for your image, bad for your mental health, bad for your physical health, or just bad people in general. If you have someone like this in your life don't hesitate to cut sling-load as you are the airframe, they are the dangerous load, so slip away from their bullshit and break contact from their immediate vicinity.

Have a plan to get out of dangerous or disadvantageous situations that leave you with some dignity. It should not be obvious that you are "breaking contact." Be prepared but remain invested. Don't have one foot out of the door the whole time or others will be able to see you're non-committal.

Chapter 38

They Will Always Be the Hero and You Will Always Be the Villain…Who Gives a Shit.

"Nobody is a villain in their own story. We're all the heroes of our own stories." – George R. R. Martin

You can be the greatest person in the world. Your integrity and morals could be beyond reproach. Anyone you meet could love you. You could be the richest person in the world, always giving to charities. You could be attending church every Sunday and feeding the homeless. You could always be right in your assertions and could be a 4.0 GPA college student working on your PhD. You could be working 3 jobs to support your family or even have been promoted the fastest within your organization. Doesn't matter. Why? Because no matter what you do, YOU will always be the villain in someone else's story.

Many people only have 1 interaction with you. That could be a positive or negative interaction and really it's irrelevant since you will most likely never see them or hear from them again. Their opinion should not be of any consequence to you.

Let's say you were driving down the highway and someone cut you off as they were trying to take the exit…which you know they saw the signs for a while back just like you did. You honk your horn to let them know you are there like most of us do but they throw up that little "gang sign" with their middle finger almost to say, or to actually say, "fuck you". You most likely did nothing wrong but to them, YOU are the reason they had to drive recklessly. YOU are the reason they decided to wait until the last minute to merge over and almost miss their exit. Nothing in their mind will compute that they themselves are the reason for almost causing the accident. It was all your fault, and if you had taken heed of their urgency, you would have made room and not had to slam on your break or honk your horn.

This is the same in many other aspects of our lives. We would be doing everything in our power to make the world a better place but all it takes is one person to ruin all of that with their actions. All we can do is shake it off and not give a shit. Who cares if we are the villain in their story. Their story probably sucks anyway and received terrible reviews on Rotten Tomatoes. We can't control others' actions of what they feel but we can control our own. Take that into account even if it pisses you off.

Being the hero of someone else's story is never going to happen. This is not a fairytale. You and I are not the be all or end all of the world. In their eyes, YOU are the villain. In your eyes, THEY are the villains. Stop caring about what others think about you and keep doing your thing…as long as your thing isn't weird or creepy…like rooting for the Dallas Cowboys. You will become much happier in the process and less stressed as a result.

Chapter 39

Everything Does Not Have to Be Explained

"Never explain – your friends do not need it and your enemies will not believe you anyway." – Elbert Hubbard

There is a thought process that says to disseminate the entire plan to those who are subordinate to you so they can complete the plan if something should happen to you. In the Army this is called the Commander's intent and is covered in an operations order.

For many things, this is a great practice and does work. Look at the airborne assault into Normandy during Operation Overlord. The majority of paratroopers did not land anywhere near their drop zone, yet the mission still got accomplished. Why? How was this feasible without direct oversight by leaders? The answer to this is that the mission was understood from the top of the command all the way to the lowest private in the assault. They could execute the mission in the Commander's absence.

Now, the planning timeline for Operation Overlord was months to years in the making and it allowed for this to be disseminated all the way down so everyone understood the plan. What I am suggesting is that this is a flexible idea. There may come times in the military, your office job, or your personal life when you must be forceful in your discretion and those entrusted to you must accept it and execute. There may not be enough time to explain the entire plan to them and time may be of the essence.

On the counter-side of that, there may be a time when you are being told to do something which you do not completely understand. You have two choices in this scenario. You can stand your ground kicking and screaming and not move until you have all the information, or you could swallow your pride and execute. This does require a certain amount of trust in the judgment of the person leading you, but if you do trust them and their thought process, following them blindly may be the right choice. Many times, things become clearer with time and what was once a misunderstood reason or mission becomes much clearer.

As a leader, you need to understand when to completely disseminate your plan or idea to your team and when to execute your plan with minimal guidance or dissemination. This requires the leader to know when these two concepts differ. It may take time to understand the nuances between them and when it crosses over. A quick flash to bang is not the normal way of things and leaders should err on the side of disseminating as much information as possible so your subordinates understand the intent.

As a subordinate, you need to realize when to shut the hell up and color. Everything doesn't always have to be explained to you. You are one spoke in the mechanism that must operate when the pedals are pressed. You do not need to know where you are going as a spoke, just know that your effort helps get the organization there. A leader's job is to give you enough information but does not include ALWAYS having to give you ALL the information. Just enough to start movement may be all that is needed. As a follower, it's up to you to trust that the person riding the bike is not riding blindly.

Chapter 40

Making Others Recognize the Value You're Providing Them

"Take time to appreciate employees and they will reciprocate in a thousand ways." – Bob Nelson

It's a tough job, doing your job day in and day out with little to no recognition. Even if you bring your A game every single day with no lapses, you may never receive the attention or praise that theoretically should come your way. Some people do it for the money, some do it for the fame, and some do it for the experience; but without anyone noticing what you have been doing, it's hard to establish yourself as a performer.

Showboating is never a good idea at work, and in fact it could backfire on you. Gloating about your past achievements is also never a good idea. Sure, it may come up in innocent enough conversations at times, but when you are the one bringing it up all the time, people start to talk, and it's probably not going to be good things.

Being a recluse is also not advised. Sure, doing your work without anyone knowing sounds great but how will they know that you are doing what you said you would do? How will they know that you are the one that's carrying others' workload? Again, boasting about yourself isn't advisable, so how can you let others know how much value you are bringing to the organization?

It's not a simple thing, but I would recommend that the best way to have others recognize the value you bring is by increasing the value *they* bring. Help others with their tasks.

Notice I did not say to do their work for them. Instead, I would pull some of this mentality from being a servant leader and ask how you can assist others with the completion of their task. Don't ask for any credit in return. Let them take it all and let them see you as the go-to person to help when they need it.

Word will eventually spread around the organization that you are approachable, easy to work with, and willing to help. It may take a little while, the message will land eventually. Additionally, you should ensure your work is done with vigor, class, and precision. Attention to the smallest details will get you noticed in the long run. Aim for perfection but be prepared to settle for very good.

Getting tasks done efficiently is a great way to show your value to others. Not just effectively. Talking up others' performance is also a great way to help others recognize what you bring to the table. Put a little extra effort on a minute detail that most would overlook. Maybe even go above and beyond for someone. There are many ways you can get yourself noticed without being self-absorbed. Let your work speak for itself, and let others speak for you. Damn, that was a good quote.

Chapter 41

Make Time. Don't Try Finding It.

"Time is more valuable than money. You can get more money, but you cannot get more time." – Jim Rohn

Trying to find time to do something seems to be how many people go about their lives these days. Sure, you can always fall back on the "I'll see if I have time" or "maybe later" but both are non-committal in nature. It shows a lack of genuine care for what's being asked of you.

Making the time for something on the other hand, shows that you actually care about the situation at hand. Instead of finding reasons NOT to do something, you intentionally find a reason TO do something. If it matters to you, it will always find a place in your schedule. If it doesn't matter to you, you are not going to waste your time with it, and the other person's time as well. It is better in this case to just tell them you do not believe you will be able to do that at this time, but if they reach back out in the future, maybe something can be worked out. Or just flat out say "no thanks."

We only have 24 hours a day to work with and it's best to use that time wisely. Let's say eight hours of it is used for sleep. That leaves us with 16 hours. Another hour is used to eat throughout the day and maybe another hour conducting hygiene. We are now down to 14 hours. If you have a 30-minute commute to and from the office, that's another hour. If you spend a lot of time on social media and relaxation, like a lot of Americans typically do, there's another few hours gone there (let's say 2–3 hours...on the lower end). Another hour is spent waiting for things to load or log on or you are on hold (computers, phone calls, etc.). That only leaves us with about 10 useful hours to use throughout the day.

Those 10 hours, if broken down into segments of 15 minutes, equals 40 time periods throughout the day in which you can actively get work done. If someone wants to shoot the shit for a few minutes, there goes 1–2 of those time blocks. If someone wants to pitch an idea to you, there goes another 1–4-time blocks. If you have a meeting there goes another 2–6-time blocks.

These time block losses add up quickly and hamper one's effectiveness and efficiency in the office. So, when someone comes to ask for something, you are sacrificing between 2.5% to 10% of your day for them. If they, or what they are telling you is important, sacrifice it by making the time because you will never find the time.

Don't go through life saying you'll have to find time to go to the gym, play with your kids, take your spouse out on a date, or do your hobby. MAKE the freaking time for the things that matter to you because you only have about 744 useful months to use in your life (that covers your age 18 to age 80), so you better make that time count for something. Stop wasting it waiting for the time to just magically appear because it won't.

Chapter 42

Just Doing Your Job Is Enough…Most of The Time…You Don't Always Have to Be The Hero

"Heroes come in all sizes, and you don't have to be a giant hero. You can be a very small hero. It's just as important to understand that accepting self-responsibility for the things you do, having good manners, caring about other people-these are heroic acts. Everybody has the choice of being a hero or not being a hero every day of their lives." – George Lucas

Showing up to work is half the job right there. Being present. Being available. Doing what you are supposed to do as dictated by your duties and scope, contract, or supervisor's direction. Just doing that is all that those managing you theoretically should expect. That IS doing your job.

As the leader, however, you have a unique skill set that has enabled you to get where you are. You may have been at the top of your class. You may have fallen into the position. Hell, you may even be the wrong person for the job. But one thing will not change until someone decides to change it...YOU are the leader.

Being in that position of authority over others has its benefits, but you need to earn them day in and day out. Resting on your laurels is not going to fly. You must earn the respect and confidence of those who rely on you, and if you're not doing all you can as the leader, you should re-evaluate your priorities.

Working your ass off is a great way to get yourself noticed, but it is a slippery slope to be climbing. You will more than likely work yourself to death before getting to where you want to be. However, this can be rectified. You don't have to be the hero all the time. Did you hear that? You, the leader, the boss, the mentor, do not always have to have the right answer. You don't always have to be the hero who saves the day. You do not have to be the one who fixes all the problems.

Sure, a cop-out can be that you are the leader, so you should know what to do, but this is a flawed philosophy.

The fact of the matter is there will come a time when you do not know what to do, where to turn, or how to respond. That is OK. You, being the good leader you are, should have people in place to help you with these things. Maybe it's your co-worker, maybe it's your deputy, maybe it's your spouse, but there is someone who can help you figure things out when you have no options.

There may be someone within your organization who knows what to do better than you. That's the person you are trying to find. That person, no matter what their official title, should have their opinion heard as well as your trusted confidant. Some of the best ideas come from those who are not necessarily the ones making the decisions. Listen to everyone and their ideas. Who knows, you might find that diamond in the rough that can push your organization to the next level right under your nose.

Let others make the decision at times and let them figure out what to do. Let your team figure out the next course of action and present you with some ideas. Their thought process might be just what you need. How they see things through their lens may vastly differ from what you see.

You, the leader, do not always have to save the day but your job is to find that person who can save the day.

Chapter 43

Know When a Personal Touch is Required

"Your plan of action is to make sure that you add that personal touch that our world is currently devoid of. The outcome will be true and will foster long lasting relationships that are free from excuses but abundant in blessings." – Farshad Asl

As one increases their level of responsibility within an organization, they will inevitably become disconnected from those they once led. The people who take care of the day-to-day business of the organization are the ones who make your plan, ideas, or vision come to life. They are where the rubber meets the road, and if you don't have a direct link to them, you may be missing out on key information that can guide your future decisions.

As I have been promoted to the next rank and level of responsibility and have changed positions, it has become harder than ever to maintain those open lines of communication with those beneath me. I have tried to make it a point to stop in each different work section every day at least once to show them I am present and available. This was the prime opportunity for me to build rapport with those I worked with and establish an open line of communication between us. The thought process is that if they see me more, their comfort level will grow and this would lead to a better understanding of what's really going on within the organization for me and my boss.

This was not meant to be seen as me spying on people, but rather a daily interaction where grievances could be aired without fear of repercussion or chastising. I would even slide some humor into the situation to help with the tense atmosphere that the military brings. This was also a two-way street where I could give them unfiltered information directly from the horse's mouth about what the plan and thought process was for myself, my boss, and my boss's boss.

This seemed to make the organization more effective, and it was something that broke up the monotony of my day and was something I looked forward to very much.

For any business, team, or organization in general, if you are a leader, here are a few tips that you could use:

Going to the actual meeting instead of your deputy

That will show others that this meeting has value and is necessary. If all you do is send your subordinates and are never there, it's obvious to others that you do not care nearly as much as they do. Show them that it is not the case. Be present for them.

Going to the location of an incident

If something happens that you did not expect and caused an issue, even if it may be dangerous, go there. Show yourself to your constituents. Show yourself to your team. Let others see you leading by example. Show no fear and be open to dialogue with those affected by the situation or incident. Find out how you can help and get their perspective.

Sending a small personal token of appreciation

These little gifts, especially if they are personalized, are a good way to show others that their accomplishments are noticed. Recognize them for what they bring to the table. Don't let their work go to waste. Show them that what they are doing is needed and valued. A handwritten note is great for this, or even a personalized email. Find some way to make those subordinate to you feel appreciated.

Giving out your personal contact information

That wall that many executives put up, known as assistants and deputies, is great for the most part at sifting through what is important and deserving of getting to the boss's desk, but it can be improved. As the leader, you have a duty to your subordinates to occasionally buck the trend and go out of your way to answer things that you don't normally answer. This will help show that you have not forgotten where you came from and to show that you yourself are human just as they are. Answer the small questions, too, not just the big ones. Your team will take notice.

A personal touch may be all that is needed at times to get the desired result. Make it a real touch, though. Mean it when you do it. Don't just go through the motions with it just because you think you should. Showing those who work for you that you are a voice that cares and that their voice matters can go a long way to ensuring the sustained success of your organization.

Chapter 44

Prior Planning Prevents Piss Poor Performance (6 P's)

"Give me six hours to chop down a tree and I will spend the first four sharpening the axe." – Abraham Lincoln

Prior planning prevents piss poor performance. The 6 P's of leadership. These six words give you a guideline for what you should expect should you not emphasize your pre-mission planning, rehearse your sales pitch, or review your class before teaching it. In other words, if you don't do what these words warn against, you will perform poorly.

We use them in the military to ensure those who are placed in charge of something never forget them. In everything we do, it comes into play. They can be applied to a training event, such as a shooting range. They can be applied to constructing a class for your superiors. They are applied at all levels of the military, from the basic Soldier all the way up to the top levels of command.

As a leader within the Old Guard, the Army's ceremonial unit stationed at Joint Base Myer-Henderson Hall in Virginia, we conducted all high-profile ceremonies that the Army and US Government had. These include burials in Arlington National Cemetery, wreath-laying ceremonies at the Tomb of the Unknown Soldier, Presidential State Funerals, Presidential Inaugurations, and Department of Defense retirement ceremonies.

Each of these particular events requires a substantial amount of planning to ensure they go off as perfectly as possible. People are told what their jobs are, Soldiers are assigned their positions in formation, spots on the ground are marked, and rehearsals are conducted. That last one is of particular importance. Rehearsing is where you make your money. Rehearse so that it becomes second nature. So that you can do it with your eyes closed. So you can be the one calling the commands. Rehearse so that you can picture the entire ceremony with your eyes closed, although if you do that on the parade field, you'll probably meet the wizard pretty quickly. IYKYK.

The planning that goes into any of these ceremonies takes months to ensure it is completely set up. There are countless nuances that cannot be accounted for until they are known. Sometimes, this does not occur until the last week before the actual ceremony, such as the case for a Presidential State Funeral. There are guest lists to be confirmed, duty assignments to be hashed out, clearances to be sought, ceremony procedures to be adjusted etc. In all of this, we must rehearse and be ready for last-minute changes.

Another aspect that needs to be understood is succession of command, or knowing who will take over your position should something happen to you. If you are not the one on the field, but you have Soldiers on the field, you need to know who will replace them if they cannot be there or something happens.

The precision that goes into a guard change at the Tomb of the Unknown Soldier is one of the most spectacular sights one can see while touring Arlington National Cemetery. The 21 steps that they take while conducting their solemn march are awe-inspiring. You can tell they put a lot of planning, rehearsal, and training into this job. The pride they had has never ceased to amaze me, and their attention to even the smallest detail of their job is something that I have taken with me and applied to other aspects of my life and career.

It is this type of attention to detail that enabled Operation Overlord to succeed during World War 2 and helped put a man on the moon.

Don't wait until the mission or decision has been made to start having a vested interest in the outcome. If you didn't care before during the planning, you don't have a right to care now.

Do the proper planning. Do the rehearsals. Know who is the next person up should you not be able to finish what you started.

Chapter 41

The Importance of the Band of Excellence

"The fundamental cause of the trouble is that in the modern world the stupid are cocksure while the intelligent are full of doubt." – Bertrand Russell

Have you ever had to deal with someone who was too smart for the job which they were filling? How about working with someone who was not intelligent enough or fit enough for that position? If you have, then those are two of the extremes that go into the band of excellence, the importance of which cannot be understated. So, what exactly is the band of excellence? It is a tool that any leader can use to ascertain whether someone is a good fit, too qualified, or underqualified for any job. It can be tailored to nearly any profession.

It is basically the balance point through which a job's duties and scope line up with the employee's abilities. Each and every job has a band of excellence. For instance, the Army in general applies this band of excellence by giving the minimum standards required for entrance to a school. It even uses it to decide whether or not someone is meeting the minimum allowable fitness standard to continue their military service.

This quasi-use of the band of excellence only focuses on the minimum standard required. It does not take into account someone who is overqualified for a job. That is the real essence of what we are talking about. Having served in the military for nearly two decades, I have come to the realization that being overqualified is nearly as bad as being underqualified.

When I would select people for special assignments, there was a happy medium that I would strive for in my interview process. It would be based upon what the job called for and subject to the limitations of the pool which I had to select from. The Army uses a "whole Soldier" concept when evaluating someone, which includes their fitness, intellectual capacity, performance, and interpersonal skills as well as a few others.

To measure fitness, we used either the Army Physical Fitness Test (APFT), Ranger Physical Fitness Test (RPFT), or the new Army Combat Fitness Test (ACFT) coupled with measuring their weight as compared to the height and overall body fat percentage.

To measure intellectual capacity, the Army used the "GT score" or general technical score. It is the ability to learn and comprehend new things and retain that knowledge, and if you scored above 110 on it you were "qualified" for most military schools and duty assignments.

To measure performance the Army used performance reviews (called OERs for officers or NCOERs for noncommissioned officers) in addition to school evaluation reports (given after attending professional development training) and counselings, which were basically just a shorter review covering a shorter period.

Finally, the interpersonal skills were measured with either peer interviews, review of the counselings, or an in-person interview before a board of reviewers with a stake in the outcome.

I would always look for a Soldier who was adequately physically fit, usually scoring above average and higher in their fitness score while being reasonably within the body fat standard with room to spare. For the performance, I would look for someone with strong reviews, not necessarily the best ones, although these were subject to interpretation. The interpersonal skills were unique in that the applicant/interviewee would be questioned on a wide variety of topics to see how well rounded their perspective was. But the easiest part, and most important aspect that I found, was applying the band of excellence to the intellectual capacity.

I would always place more emphasis on a Soldier that scored between 100 to 120 points on this scale. Anything lower than that, and they, more often than not, would not have the intelligence to perform the duty I was asking of them. For those that scored well above 120 points, they were often too analytical in their approach and took too long to actually act. This is not to say those who scored lower or those who scored higher were bad candidates since there are always those who buck the trend, but when time is of the essence, using a tool such as this made my job much easier.

I'd suggest using this after figuring out what qualities are pertinent to the job. Mine was useful for my job as a senior leader in the Army. It is probably not useful for a banker or professional football scout. Take the time actually to know what matters to you and your organization and you will save a lot of time on the back end.

Chapter 46

Be the Steward

"The difference between ownership and stewardship is that you can do what you want with what you own. When you become a steward, you recognize that you have just as much control as an owner, but a responsibility that's greater than yourself." – Josh Steimle

Being a steward means you take ownership of an organization while not being the owner and ensure it is successful for those in the future. In the military, this is true for everyone, as the turnover within is so vast. Sure, some may only complete a short 3–4-year contract, but there is still a significant portion that pushes forward to reach that retirement age. Both sets of these individuals have their roles to play in being stewards for the next generation of Soldiers. In these cases, it means ensuring that everything within their unit is maintained and that the assigned personnel know what to do in any situation.

Being a leader within the organization, you must be able to balance the lifestyle required of both. Leaders accomplish missions by any means necessary. Stewards ensure the organization can flourish well into the future and hold it in trust for the next generation. As a leader in the military or within any organization, for that matter, you must be able to do both. Any fluctuation of being more one than the other and you will have different results in outcome, some of which may not be advantageous.

For instance, let's say the leader inside you decides to put all effort and resources into one objective or plan. You totally commit yourself, your men, and your equipment to accomplish that task. There's not very much stewardship going on in this case. The future is being ignored as a result, and if the mission should fail, the future might be uncertain. There are times when this is necessary, such as when the tempo or massing of forces is necessary, but it is not the norm. When this is done, there is a significant amount of risk to the leader if the mission does not turn out as intended, and he may have left himself vulnerable to the enemy or missed an opportunity due to a lack of resources.

The point of being the steward is ensuring you, your subordinates, and the organization can continue operating no matter what happens. This means you must know those who work for you and what makes them tick. You must know the equipment you are using and its lifecycle. You must know how tasks within a job affect others doing that job, and you must ensure you can balance the personal lives of those working for you with the organization's demands.

You are not larger than the mission at hand. You are not bigger than the organization. You must ensure the job can be done for as long as possible. It's a job of give and take. Push and pull. Exercise and Rest. Giving your all when it's called for, but also relaxing when the time is right.

Take your breaks. Take your time off. Take your sick days. Take a longer lunch occasionally. But also put in the damn work. Stay late if you must. Ask more from others at times, but also take the load off them at times.

Be the steward!

Your organization will benefit from it and you will become a better person for it. Just because you're not the owner does not mean you should not have an interest in the success of your business, team, or organization.

Chapter 47

Treat the Problem, Not the Symptoms

"Deal With the Cause, Not the Symptom." – Anne Dennish

Doctors treat symptoms and underlying problems. They use those symptoms to diagnose issues and see patterns. That is what leaders need to do as well. It is not enough to always make quick fixes to things. Being reactive is not going to work well for longevity, even if it does show calmness under pressure. The symptoms do need to be addressed, but if that is the only thing that you, as the leader, are doing, you will always be playing catch up. Proactivity and fixing the source of the problem are what really need to be done.

Pay attention to why certain things are always late. Pay attention to who is at a friction point in the process. Pay attention to complaints about the same person again and again. These can be used as indicators of a larger problem within your organization. If these small things are ignored, they do eventually take a toll on the workforce and organization at large.

The occasional lateness or misstep by an employee is not of concern, but should the frequency increase, there might be something that the leader should at least inquire about. Leaders are inherently problem solvers, and that's a good thing. But if all you are doing is solving problems, you are only ever going to be a problem solver...not a leader.

If you receive complaints from numerous employees about a certain supervisor, address those complaints. This may be a simple discussion or maybe something a little stronger, such as disciplinary actions or even having to fire or reassign someone.

If you notice that some paperwork is frequently late, figure out the chain of custody, and you will find your issue. You may find someone in the chain who shouldn't be there or that someone is erroneously applying a metric.

The solution may not always be to fire someone, it may also be that you need to fix your system or even hire an additional employee. Maybe employee training needs to be conducted, or hours must be re-evaluated. There is never going to be a cookie-cutter answer to finding the actual problem, but if all you do is treat the symptoms of that problem, you are never going to find the cure.

Chapter 48

Control What You Can Control

"You cannot control the behavior of others, but you can always choose how you respond to it." – Roy T. Bennett

You are not God. There are things that, no matter how hard you try, you will never be able to affect or control the outcome of. This can be a hard pill to swallow as a leader. Not having the ability to make certain things happen is something that true leaders must learn to cope with.

Control what you can control. That starts with your actions, words, thoughts, deeds, appearance, etc. Make good decisions. Take advice. Control your emotions and keep them in check. Listen to those who have walked in your shoes before. Follow the paths set forth by those before you.

I can influence people all day long. I can provide my expert opinion (if you can call it that) and give someone else all the tools they need to succeed. I can fill your gas tank but can't make you drive. I can be available for you day and night, but I can't be the one to make the call for help. That falls on someone else. That someone else is not me therefore, I cannot control it.

Have some faith in your team after you let them go. If you have given them a proper briefing, given strong guidance, and provided them with all the tools they need to succeed, let go of the reins. It's no longer in your control. If it is still in your control, you are not the leader. If you can't let go of the reins, you must re-evaluate your position within that organization. You might have to look again at how well you train your team since you don't trust them enough to make decisions or complete the task.

There are absolutely times when the expert (leader) needs to take over, but this should not be the norm. The leader should be the master of delegation until those who can be delegated to are not capable of accomplishing the task at hand. Delegate, then follow up with them. Don't just send off the email without following up.

Remember, there is only a small portion that you can actually control, but it starts from within yourself. Be in control.

Chapter 49

Known Knowns, Known Unknowns, Unknown Unknowns, Unknown Knowns

"Knowing what you don't know is the beginning of wisdom." – Debasish Mridha.

He may be a controversial figure, but Donald Rumsfeld had some interesting talking points concerning these different 'knowns,' although I don't think he expressed them appropriately.

Known knowns are things that you know that you should know. An example of this would be knowing that your job needs you to do a certain thing, and you know what it is and how to do it. It's completely out in the open, and most people would also recognize it.

A known unknown is something that you do not know the answer to, but you do know that you need to figure it out. An example would be when one of your teammates asks you for help with a situation that does not have a clear-cut answer or a dilemma where any answer has some problems. You know that you do not know, but you are also aware it is a problem needing a solution.

An unknown unknown is something you don't even know is a problem because it is not apparent to you or has never come up before. It is the things within our jobs that are so random or unapparent that one cannot even conceive of them or be able to label them. They have never come up before, so no one has ever thought to figure them out.

Finally, an unknown known is something you perceive to be true, but it turns out to be false. An example would be thinking that the Dallas Cowboys are a good football team. But in a much more real sense, this can be something that has been a constant your whole career and recently changed, unbeknownst to you. This can include many things, such as new laws, regulations, standards, or interaction protocols. Coming to terms with what you once thought was correct, only to find out it was always or is now wrong, can be a tough pill to swallow, but true leaders need to recognize this and accept it.

Why are these things important to a leader?

As a leader within an organization and at any level, you must be aware of your and your subordinates' limitations – a seemingly major issue that you find may not have even registered on their radar as being important, that they may not have even thought about. It's your job as the leader to notice this and break things down for shared understanding between all team members.

As discussed earlier, you need to be humble about the things you do not know yourself and be empathetic to those filling the shoes you used to fill. Just because something is glaringly obvious to you does not mean it is to them. It may mean that you may not have done your job making things such as the problem at hand a known known to them.

It's your job as a leader to change all the unknowns into knowns. If you fail at this, the blame is not on your people for not knowing, it is on you for not articulating it in a way that they understand. You may need to adjust your communication style. Think about it.

Chapter 50

Don't Grab the Monkey

"If I have to always do your damn job, I do not need you." – Literally every leader at one time or another in the military

It's not your job to fix all the problems your team has. Their dilemmas should not become yours just because they can't determine which way to go. William Oncken, in his *Harvard Book Review* (HBR) publication, advocated for this in his paper entitled, "Management Time: Who's Got the Monkey?" When you continuously take over for your team's shortcomings, you will inevitably make them reliant on you, thus making them useless. Don't volunteer to do your subordinate's job. They work for you. You do not work for them, even though you should give them the tools they need to succeed.

With each position I have held in my career, I have had this happen more often than I'd like to admit. I have even been the one who was relied upon to make a plan happen. I was the mallet that pushed the square peg through the round hole at times and had taken over for my team's inexperience or incompetence a lot more than I should have. This is one of the crappy things about being a leader. I have also been the person who had to have their boss take over for them due to inefficiency at times. No one is perfect...not even me...even though my dog would think otherwise.

Once you establish yourself as reliable and efficient, you start to get more things assigned to you since you can be trusted to get them done. This will eventually lead to you becoming overburdened, and since your team will get to their breaking point sooner than you, your team will start to rely on you more and more to give them the answers to the test. You will get to the point where you are doing the work that your team should be doing. You do not want to fail, so you do it begrudgingly.

Do not fall into this downward spiral. Keep your team accountable for their own pieces of the pie. Assign them tasks and give them deadlines. Tell them to bring you a plan for that issue they are having, even if it's a dumb plan. You can then start working through solutions with them without starting from scratch. Who knows, they may even figure it out without you doing it for them. Once you hold them accountable for themselves, they will surprise you with their ingenuity and resourcefulness. They don't want to fail, either. Or at least they shouldn't want to.

There will be times when it saves time to take the monkey off your subordinates' back and place it on your own. It may save time, resources, and even a business plan, but it should be the last resort as a leader. You are paid to get things done and keep the machine working. You are not paid to do other people's jobs but to make them do theirs. Their shortcomings or inexperience can be amended by additional training, guidance, or mentorship. By taking on other people's tasks and making them your own, you are lowering yourself and lessening the impact you can have on the organization at large. Give assignments, provide guidance, give deadlines, and follow up. It's not your monkey to carry. It's theirs. Make them carry it.

Afterword

While the insights found within this book are things I have learned throughout my career, they are not the be all or end all. There are countless more tools, tips, tricks, and things that help make us all better at our jobs, in our families, and as a person. I am certain that a lot of this material within these pages has reminded each of you about an issue you had where you did not have the right answer. I am also certain that while none of this is brand new, it will have sparked some critical thinking on your part on how to become a better leader.

This book is the essence of what it means to be everyone except the person at the top, even though they can also benefit from knowing these techniques. We are all leading in a sense, while also having someone else lead us. It's our job to do our best to be as impactful and efficient as possible. No, you are not the leader. No, you will most likely never be THE leader. But that does not mean that you cannot impact those around you by being a led leader.

Show others how by emulating what you want them to be.

Be the example for them to mirror.

It's okay to never be the top dog but that does not mean you don't get to eat.

Acknowledgments

There are a significant number of people I would like to thank for helping me finally get this finished. God, my wife, my kids, my family, extended family, friends, acquaintances, co-workers, supervisors, subordinates...Damn near everyone I have ever had an interaction with.

I'm still working on this aspect of my life and I wish it was a larger part of me but without God's guidance and keen eye watching over my family, this book would not have been possible.

To my wife, thank you for putting up with my crap over the last 17 years. Without your support and love, the kindness you show everyone, and pushing me to be a better person, I would have never been able to complete this. I love your face.

To my kids, you guys are awesome. I never thought that God would bless me with six little people to keep alive. You make every single day exciting, even when you are yelling and fighting with each other, and not going to bed when you are told, or not showering when you are told, or not eating when you are told, or not doing your chores...I think you get the point. All of you make the work I do worth it. I love you.

To my mom, dad, brothers, and sister, thank you all for being behind me all the time. No really, I'm literally faster than all of you. You guys made me the person I am today. I hope this book makes you proud. I love you all.

To my extended family and friends, every one of you no matter how insignificant a part you think you've played in my life, have made this book happen. From our interactions to the insight and guidance you have given me. Thank you all. I love you guys.

To everyone else I have had the pleasure of knowing (unless you're a Dallas Cowboys fan...well, even some of you are good people), thank you for putting up with my crap and helping me get here. Yes, even if you sucked as a leader (and there are many), or thought I sucked (of whom there are just as many), I probably learned something from you, even if it's what not to do.

About the author

Sean Sweeney was born in Philadelphia, PA in 1986 and enlisted in the Army in 2004, just a few months after his 18th birthday. He is currently a United States Army Senior Noncommissioned Officer (NCO) with over 18 years of military service. Recently selected to attend the Army's Sergeants Major Academy, he has performed duties in all noncommissioned officer positions up to and including a Company First Sergeant in units ranging from special operations, light infantry, airborne, mechanized, and ceremonial. He has been assigned to Fort Benning, Georgia; Fort Riley, Kansas; Fort Jackson, South Carolina; Vicenza, Italy; Joint Base Myer-Henderson Hall, Virginia; University of Houston; and Fort Bliss, Texas. He has been deployed four times, including combat tours to both Afghanistan and Iraq, and has trained in numerous countries across Europe and Southwest Asia. Sean is married to his wife, Heather, and they have six (yes, SIX) children and reside in El Paso, TX. He holds a Master's degree in Business Administration (Strategic Management) and is currently a Doctoral student working towards a Doctor of Business Administration (Leadership) degree while simultaneously attending class 74 of the United States Army Sergeants Major Academy.